"a dirty hand"

Winfield Townley Scott

Poetry, music, I have loved, and yet . . .
I bend my body to the spade
Or grope with a dirty hand.

Yeats

The Literary Notebooks of
Winfield Townley Scott

"a dirty hand"

Foreword by Merle Armitage

UNIVERSITY OF TEXAS PRESS, AUSTIN & LONDON

ACKNOWLEDGMENTS

GRATITUDE IS expressed to A. P. Watt and Sons, Ltd., The Macmillan Company of London, Mr. Michael Butler Yeats, and The Macmillan Company of New York for permission to use as an epigraph three lines of "The Spirit Medium" from *Collected Poems* by William Butler Yeats, © 1940 by Georgie Yeats, renewed 1968 by Bertha Georgie Yeats, Anne Yeats, and Michael Butler Yeats; to Doubleday and Company, Inc., and Mrs. Winfield Townley Scott for permission to quote two stanzas of "Electric Silence" from *New and Selected Poems* by Winfield Townley Scott, © 1967 by Prescott College Press; and to New Directions Publishing Corporation and Mrs. William Carlos Williams for permission to reprint "The Red Wheelbarrow" from *The Collected Earlier Poems of William Carlos Williams,* © 1938 by William Carlos Williams.

Design and Typography

By Merle Armitage

Standard Book Number 292-78416-3
Library of Congress Catalog Card No. 71-77470
Copyright © 1969 by Mrs. Winfield Townley Scott
Manufactured in the United States of America

To

Anne Hutchens McCormick

and

Samuel S. Vaughan

Yet, though now of Muse bereft,
I have still the manners left
. . . who only can
Be in prose a grateful man.
                                        Herrick

FOREWORD

IN THE GUEST HOUSE of Eleanor and Winfield Scott's home in Santa Fe, two large loose-leaf notebooks lay on the table in my room. This was actually a work-table for Winfield, who frequently used the room to escape the dynamic glee of his children. For days I glanced at them, and on one Sunday morning, with everyone else asleep, I decided to invade privacy and was immediately engaged.

Here were extraordinary thoughts written by a rare mind and heart, a poet's nature as it responded to the world and everything in it. There were penetrating analyses of writers, of personalities, of eccentrics, and of their influences. It was surely a find, and I was elated and anxious to talk with Winfield about this new aspect of his writing. Of course it was obvious that these were private observations, very private indeed.

At breakfast that Sunday morning we had an animated conversation about these notes, and I made a strong plea for their publication. Although he was very pleased, he sought to discourage me by insisting they were just dinner table conversation pieces, but I demurred, maintaining that they were penetrating observations of real importance and would have a wide interest. He insisted that they never be published until his death.

But my enthusiasm did cause him to re-edit them, bring them up to date, and have them expertly typed. And I kept them very much in mind. Winfield Townley Scott was a major poet who also wrote some very discerning criticism, and in these notes we see another aspect, an important dimension of this gifted man.

It is impossible to read the poetry of Winfield Scott without feeling an expansion of one's sympathies. He enlarges our vision and sharpens both our observations and our discriminations. He often recalls half-forgotten images concealed in our subconscious, which then come to light with a curiously physical force.

You can taste the salt of the sea in many of his New England poems, and some have the color of weather-beaten unpainted barns, or the pungent nets of fishermen. Yet his Southwestern poems and essays are redolent with the smoke of pinyon fires. He evokes the shimmering pauses of autumn, the ancient mysteries of the Indians, the color of their kachinas. He possessed a positive intuition for nuances.

His poetry can be extremely poignant without recourse to sentimentality or any other cheap device. The death of President Kennedy was possibly the most agonizing experience for Winfield. I was with the Scott family during those calamitous days, and his grief was paralyzing. This traumatic experience later produced one of the noble poems, a five-stanza outpouring of grief which he titled: "Electric Silence." The last two of the five stanzas are:

> From the gush of red roses in the car
> To the useless hospital
> To the flags in the wind
> To the horses' clatter
> To the drums the drums the drums
> To the silent flame
> The autumn night swiftly over all.
>   That hurtful peace.

O with his Irish that night, we cried-down the rain.

Scott was born in 1910 in Haverhill, Massachusetts, for his mother had traveled home to her family doctor. He lived in Newport, Rhode Island, until he was ten. During his late grammar school and high school years he lived in Haverhill. Then to Providence, Rhode Island, for four years of college (Brown) and twenty years as a newspaperman on the Providence *Journal*. This work included book reviews which brought him national attention.

He and his family came to Santa Fe, New Mexico, on a tour that promised to take them all over the West, but Santa Fe was such a new and arresting environment that they decided to remain for a while and enjoy the enchantments of New Mexico. They never returned East, except for brief visits. One of his most perceptive and poetic essays is concerned with the Indian, Spanish, and adobe characteristics of this ancient city and its environs.

His *Collected Poems: 1937–1962* (The Macmillan Co., 1962) includes most of the contents of the preceding seven books. Other works include a book of essays, *Exiles and Fabrications* (Doubleday, 1961). His final book of poetry, *New and Selected Poems,* edited by George P. Elliott, was published by Doubleday in 1967. He is included in many anthologies. He received honorary degrees from Rhode Island College and the University of New Mexico.

Scott's sympathies in poets and poetry were discerning but wide, and he and his wife attracted friends of the most catholic and diverse interests. Their home was a rendezvous for notables in every category as they traveled across the continent. They shared their hospitality with William Primrose, Thornton Wilder, William Carlos Williams, and hosts of others who delighted in this old-fashioned, unpretentious salon. It was an atmosphere of utter relaxation, and formidable figures often expressed themselves on politics, art, music, and literature as among close and trusted friends.

Scott was not identified with any particular group or movement. The evocative quality of his writing is strong in both his poetry and his essays. Often his writing is as personal, as individual, and as identifiable as are the paintings of Paul Klee. Much of his poetic power is in his ability to express the inexpressible, and he accomplishes this in terms which are unforgettable.

He was a warm human being, sensitive, always moved by the happy or tragic circumstances attending his friends. He was shy. He once said to me: "I wish I could tell you how much I owe you for your encouragement. I suppose I have a Yankee streak that shies me off the very praise I, like most writers, love to have. I have over and over again watched myself in such encounters, trying as soon as possible to change the subject of conversation."

His own Providence *Journal* summed up the loss of Winfield Townley Scott in an editorial in the issue of Sunday, May 5th, 1968. It is headed:

W.T.S.

(1910–1968)

and reads:

At first there is the stunned shock, the disbelief. Then the sense of sudden—and personal—loss, as though a large part of one's own life has gone with him. And so it has. Then the resentment that can't be reasoned away—not yet, not yet—at the way the universe is run.

He should have lived as long as Frost, as long as William Carlos Williams. He was busy, he was writing well, better than ever before, as the new poems in the last collection showed. From the beginning, his voice had always been his own—singular, unmistakable—and as the years passed it gathered strength, gained an added authority and control in every way he used it, from the short and singing lyrics to the long narrative poems. He should have lived because there was so much for him to see and say. Yes, and Camus should have lived as long as Hugo, and Fitzgerald as long as Hemingway, and Dylan Thomas as long as Yeats—and this was not the way of it.

So the writings remain, and the memories of the man (memories that bring with them, as they must, a faint and aromatic whiff of pipe-smoke); the soft voice, the chuckle, the eloquence with which he read aloud the poems of the writers he loved, the Yankee stoniness of his anger when faced with deeds or words that seemed to demean or diminish the humane values that civilized man must live by, the warmth of his humor, his generosity, his enthusiasms.

In American literature, his name and the impact of his work will continue to grow. But a friend has gone, and to learn to live with the loss will be a long time coming.

This tribute speaks for Winfield's many friends—including those who never met him. In his poems, in his prose writings, and in his life he moved gracefully, always talking of what mattered to him. He assumed, modestly, generously, that it mattered to his audience, too. And it did.

Manzanita Ranch   Merle Armitage
Yucca Valley, California

"a dirty hand"

POETRY—the most concentrated use of language.

●

PEOPLE who say they don't like—or don't understand—"modern poetry": ask them what poetry they *do* like and understand. They are lying and lazy, invariably. Their implication that Shakespeare, for instance, is all clear daylight to them is certain to be hypocrisy.

●

FRANK LLOYD WRIGHT'S: There is no such thing as "modern architecture"—there is *architecture*. Same thing for poetry.

●

FRANCES MINTURN HOWARD said to me that while the audience for poetry is pitifully small, those who do care for poetry care so intensely that it seems to make up the difference.

3

ALWAYS REMEMBER Wassili Leps's remark when S. said she didn't care for music: "Why do you *like* to say that?"

•

STILL—OF COURSE—there are people soaked in, say, Victorian poetry; maybe Browning especially; and they give every evidence of enjoying and (I suppose) "understanding" it; and they are quick, in the name of what they do like, to dismiss "modern poetry." In other words, they speak for some love and knowledge of poetry and with apparent sincerity. One must say of them that they are able to care for one or two kinds of poetry and there they stop. It is much better than nothing. But they do confuse their limitation of taste with intellectual disapproval. If they should read backwards into, say, the seventeenth-century metaphysicals they would again be ill at ease; probably not so vocally because Donne et al. *are* in the books. Such readers respect the established. What they want art to do is go on conforming to itself as of a particular phase or period: the one thing art cannot do and stay alive. (They will deny all this.)

•

IT IS SILLY to say one likes "modern poetry." My God, the verse committed to print month after month is largely bad. No doubt this is always true—in any era and of any art.

•

AS A POET one does—simply—the best one can. This is something. Contrast those who work for hire.

4

ROBERT WILSON—socio-psychologist at Harvard—has been interviewing a couple of dozen poets. He told me one of his general conclusions was that no other professional group thinks so frequently in terms of posthumous reputation. Wilson also observed that there is no standard of measurement of a poet's success: it's all a matter of opinion and opinion keeps varying. And there of course is the explanation of the poet's seeming vanity for fame after death—there and in the multiple examples in past history of the neglected, underestimated, misunderstood, even the unknown, resurrected to immortality.

●

POUND, SOMEWHERE in his published *Letters*, asserts that a lifetime given to poetry is justified if only half a dozen of one's lines survive. That's immortality, says Pound. I think he wrote this when he was still quite young, too.—I remember when I was college age, Harry Hurd said one day he'd be glad if he could leave just one poem that would stay in the anthologies. That seemed to me an almost shockingly modest desire—then.—There is a poem by Emerson about how can a poet tell which of all his lines may be the few lasting ones.

●

EMERSON'S POEMS seem admirable if you like the wood left a little rough, as I do. As though reality—integrity—were proved. For me, above all, Thomas Hardy's poems. They fumble and stumble into poetry; as though in spite of themselves. How else could they get their particular emotional effects? which are so

5

profound. Of course I mean his—to me—"best poems." One always means that. I know Yeats said Hardy's poetry was admired because people no longer cared about art; but that is just one kind of poet commenting on another kind—it doesn't signify.

●

I AM TRYING to put down things I have thought—collecting them as well as I can remember; and then to go on, adding. It is more fun than writing essays; arrangement, progression, transition, are hard for me to manage. (Though here the disconnections may often be semi.)

●

ONCE I LEARNED from a Governor of Rhode Island a good thing about writing: Theodore Francis Green said never comment on the way your are expressing yourself. —Which reminds me I hate the word "frankly." Use it, and immediately you arouse suspicions as to your complete honesty. —I have never succeeded wholly in following Mr. Green's precept.

●

QUOTATION MARKS are frequently comment: see, I am using slang. Thus: We had a "hot tip" from one of the "kids." Horrible, vulgar. Never, never. Contrast Mark Twain's style. Recall Emerson's (wistful?) remark on the language of the street: Like bullets. An artist does not quote it: he uses it.

6

SINCERITY. When I was a youngster, but already far gone in ambition to be a writer, I read that Joseph Conrad said sincerity was the great thing. That, I thought, is that: I am very sincere. Unfortunately it took me many years to discover how extraordinarily difficult it is to write sincerely. With all the will toward sincerity, we are nonetheless monsters of self-deception; and one's self-deception involves everybody one knows. . . . I must try to come back to this. It is a large matter.

•

ONE REASON for writing these notes: I love to read this sort of thing when somebody else writes it. Almost, I think, no matter who.

•

YEARS AND YEARS ago I also read John Erskine had said that for a man to write a good novel he must not only have the ability to write, he must also have a philosophy of life. As a youngster I was depressed by my inadequacy; at forty, I still am. (Not that I want to write novels.)

•

I MUST TRY not to try to be smart in these notes. I must bear in mind that that wouldn't be the point.

•

PEOPLE ARE forever saying things about writing which one recalls over and over. William Saroyan's advice that you should

7

sit down to write as though you were the only writer in the world. Charles Jackson's charming recollection that when he wrote his first poems, in his adolescence, he would rush to a mirror to see if his looks had changed.

●

DOES ONE EVER come to feel wise, or even mature, or even adult? —Dreiser once told an interviewer that young men suppose that somewhere along in life everything gets calm—in its place—all right; it never happens, said Dreiser.

●

"WHATSOEVER THE MORNING saith unto you, do that." Thus—I think I quote correctly—Emerson. And then you find his neighbor Thoreau, I think in a poem, crying out at his own neglect of, or the dangers to, his "morning wishes." This image arises straight from fact and common experience: the sense of newness, of ambition, of rest and readiness, of integrity, of beginning again. (In a poem called "Memorabilia" I consciously stole from Emerson: "What the morning says to do.")

●

WILLIAM FAULKNER was quoted in the papers the other day as saying each of his books seemed to him to fail, he remained dissatisfied with what he had done. An artist. Compare Dorothy Wellesley's alarm when Yeats told her he thought he was at last learning how to write—and this was, in fact, just before Yeats's death at seventy-three.

●

THE BAROQUE STYLE. Elliot Paul in a letter to me said H. P. Lovecraft's style always reminded him of a cartload of bananas.

●

THAT GREAT principle of writing which Mark Twain enunciated so simply: Don't say the old lady screamed—bring her on and let her scream.

●

I REMEMBER that D. H. Lawrence warned Amy Lowell against comparing big things with small. That is, in her imagery: as (I'm improvising) saying the sun is like a sunflower. He was right. Imagery must open up, not diminish. Write contrary to his advice, and you write pretty, petty, special—or, to roll it all up in one word, sentimental. This is one of the things I put down because it has stayed in my mind.

●

MAY ONE SAY that the effort of all art is to *fix* meanings? Not, of course, to "make"—living has meanings without art. But to *fix.* . . . Axel Dorner says: "tension and mutability"—that these are the characteristics of modern life and they therefore will be of any significant art. No absolutes. I think I understand this and in a way agree. But always there comes to my mind Frost's remark that a poem is "a momentary stay against confusion." I feel —simply, directly, from experience—the truth of Frost's remark, and I am trying to determine if it contradicts Dorner's theory (which, intellectually, I find appealing).

•

TODAY I HAVE been reading several new books of poetry—having delayed, put them off, for weeks because (except for the really poor stuff) they ask so much of the reader: so much concentration; so much orientation as you confront another unfamiliar mind. Poems long known may be a pleasure to read when you are tired—but never new poems: they demand, as I say, too much. This of course points to the great power of poetry; this is a sort of tribute. But if I feel this effort—who have read and tried to write poetry for twenty-five years—is it any wonder, after all, that the general reader runs away? I don't compliment him, but I understand his reaction. . . . In this connection, you can see the explanation for the comparative popularity of poets who work wholly in the traditions; they merely repeat what has been done before and readers feel comfortable—at home—with them. No impurity of personal stamp in the poetry—no necessity for fresh seeing on the part of the reader. . . . But how sad it is that contemporary poetry is mostly ignored by the general reader. More specifically, I mean the intelligent, pretty well educated man and woman who read much of the new non-fiction, many of the articles in the better magazines, and a number of the best new novels. Altogether, such readers would make an infinitely larger audience for poetry than it has. But they don't read it. Note that this is reflected in such magazines as *Harper's* and *The Atlantic*: the verse there published is nearly always tamer than the articles—asks less of the reader.

●

REMEMBER WHAT Edith Sitwell said, years ago: poetry is an art—not a dumping ground for the emotions.

●

TWO OR THREE things I heard Wallace Stevens say a couple of weeks ago in New York where he was answering literary editors' questions. He said that if he had not had to earn his living he would have done nothing but write poetry. Dismissing *what* a poet does for a living, he said how "fortuitous is the choice" of any profession. He said, "Unless you write about things in a literal sense, you won't write poetry."

●

TO START a poem—the necessary tone. Usually a phrase, a line, which will, apparently, set the style—suggest the syntax, the movement. An "idea" for a poem will not, I find, move until this happens. Sometimes the phrase comes first—that is easiest, then. When the "idea" comes first—and this is the more frequent experience as I get older—one often waits a long time for the language; and sometimes in vain.

THE COMMONEST, falsest trick of youngsters and amateurs in poetry is to get a booming "last line" and build a poem to set it up on. —This is also done by false poets; cf. George Sterling and such obvious wind as "between the thunder and the sun." . . . By the way, though it isn't the same thing of course, consider also the repetitive grand climaxes so frequent in music. Exciting as they often are, one may suppose one is being had. —In poetry the diminuendo finish becomes increasingly attractive.

•

READING A GROUP of poems by the "Activists," and founder Lawrence Hart's statement of principles: strip to image and phrase, association, automatism. All right—the results are pretty lively. It sounds as though Hart discovered good ways of teaching. But the end result will not be great unless one or another of these poets, absorbing and outgrowing these principles, becomes a great poet. Imagism—Vorticism—Activism—always this sort of endeavor starts toward liberation and knots up into limitation. . . . Fifteen years ago on the west coast it was Yvor Winters: all strict rhyme and meter, all impersonality, all neo-classicism and anti-romantic: only way to write poetry. Winters whipped himself and his group like a dedicated, solemn sado-masochist. And what came of it all? Nothing. . . . Cannot one declare that all poetic composition which proceeds directly from critical theory remains illustrative and not creative? —Now, I know the value of the critical faculty and I know the sentimental waste of the supposition that poetry just comes naturally. Of course. But this is enough here, unless I want to get into an essay, which I don't.

RECENTLY IN a superficial roundup on new books of poetry I printed a generality or two which I want to save. For one thing, I said that poets who write in traditional forms *in familiar ways* seem to suffer—despite all their frequent buoyancy—a kind of fatigue, and that poetry never survives fatigue.

•

I QUESTIONED Eliot's pronouncement, which Auden applauded, that the most promising aspect of a young poet's work is his craftsmanship, "for it is evidence," says Auden, "of a capacity for detachment from the self and its emotions without which no art is possible." This sounds sensible, and certainly one doesn't want shoddy work or the personal messiness. But in fact, I have noticed, precocious maturity in craftsmanship most often occurs in poets who do not develop; usually they cease and disappear. On the other hand, poets who do develop are most often among those who stumble and grope through their beginnings: in search, each, of himself or—to use Frost's word—his *difference* from others. . . . Am I generalizing in the interests of self-justification? Very likely.

•

FINALLY, I ASKED why the development of such a poet as Auden seemed to be in the direction of light verse? And I did not try to answer my question. I still don't feel that I can formulate a clear, satisfactory answer. But I think Auden's cleverness, his cerebration and skill, his self-projection in many roles, all thrust him into impersonality which, like it or not, is not fruitful for a poet; and this I think has to do with his touching his materials more and more distantly, lightly. Lack of self-involvement leads to humor. . . . Oh, yes: I also said, in another instance, that the cool young poet seemed so noncommital he seemed uncommitted. The crack may apply here.

•

SOME YEARS ago the appearance of one of these groups—this-is-the-way-to-do-it—with all its apparent assurance would have panicked me or at least disturbed me. Now, no. —And yet how long it has taken me to learn that each of us has to find his own way and that there is no substitute for self.

•

IT IS CONSTANTLY remarked that the American audience for poetry is infinitesimal. What is astounding, though, is how often the remark—how almost always the remark—is assumed to be a criticism of poetry.

•

WORDS ARE very powerful. You aren't sure of that? —Think of all the things you won't say.

•

GLANCING AT Frost's *Poems*. They are yet to be studied, to be really written about. The approach might be to read carefully the inferior ones—the ones you always skip over as you go from familiar and famous page to f. and f. page; in the poor ones you probably would find, clear, the limitations which (less easy to catch amid the victories) mar the best; and thus begin to define him—to place and judge him. . . . Inadvertently, I have proffered a modification to the old saw that "a poet is judged by his best poems." Perhaps one would better say: he is appraised by his best poems. —Take, as one easy example, Keats: he is estimated —appraised—ranked—by his best poems; but a judgment of him would be false—a description, a conception, an understanding of him would be false—which was so selective. . . . I don't think I'm merely befooled here with a semantics game. I am trying to isolate, in the case of Frost, the approach which will *clarify* the significance of a particular body of work; (and which has not at all been clarified in Frost's case). . . . I will bet that his significance is minor and enduring.

•

GLANCING AT E. A. Robinson—after years of scarcely (deliberately not) reading him. I begin to feel objective—to think I could manage a Matthew Arnold-on-Wordsworth. . . . Out of fifteen hundred or more pages, the permanent residue is bound to be a minority. But the little I looked at—it was his *Sonnets*— made me happy; for the best things had even improved, and some unnoticed things suddenly were profound. . . . I am older: what other test is there?

•

LINDSAY (ELEVEN) had been to see a movie of Kipling's *Kim*; and later I saw him fingering a copy of the book from a shelf near my desk. I said, "Don't you want to read it?" and he said, "No; it might spoil the movie for me." . . . I record this as a literary note on the younger generation and our times. (But I have never read *Kim* and I didn't see the movie.)

•

THE SCULPTOR Waldemar Raemisch told me that he tells his students to read the biographies of great artists. Yes. It is the way to be reminded of standards—of uncompromising devotion to one's self. The only way for the artist. You either have it or you don't. . . . Do I sound as though I think I have it? Do you think you have it? —Remember Joan of Arc. Her wily judges asked her if she were in God's grace; for if she claimed she was, she branded herself an apostate, and equally if she confessed she was not, she branded herself as damned. She replied: "If I am not, may God put me there; and if I am, may God so keep me. I should be the saddest creature in the world if I knew I were not in His grace."

•

LEE ANDERSON told me that Auden wagged a finger at him across a luncheon table and said, "Don't condescend to Tennyson: he was the finest technician in English poetry." . . . This interests me because of my notion that Auden is to our era what Tennyson was to his; even though Auden is not as good a poet.

IN *A Child's Garden of Verses:*

> The Dog, and the Plough, and the Hunter, and all
> And the star of the sailor, and Mars,
> These shone in the sky, and the pail by the wall
> Would be half full of water and stars.

NOTE: "half full." Why is it so good? I think, because here is sentimental flight of fancy, and the exactitude—the restriction—the *modesty* of the qualifying phrase assume a reality we cannot question. Instead, we are immensely pleased and charmed, and wholly believing.

•

WHENEVER I MEET a clergyman, I know I am to discover, pretty quickly, the answer to one question: Is he a hypocrite or a fool? The fools—when not embarrassingly stupid—are sometimes sweet and likeable men; the hypocrites never. This judgment is equally true of those literary people who can be classed as either fourflushers or self-deceivers; one can never abide the fake; but one often finds admirable sincerity in the pathetically small-talented. I mean: one can condone delusion but never the cynical program to delude others. . . . In fact I think sincerity always admirable, even if insane.

•

IT IS VERY foolhardy—perhaps impossible—to write poetry about exceptional things. Beware of glorious sunsets.

READING OVER some of these paragraphs, I noticed: "Lack of self-involvement leads to humor." There I may have blundered on an abstraction which explains an observation I made—not uniquely, God knows: but really finding it out (the truest way) in my own experience—years ago: that one writes best humorously when one is depressed. (Sad. Sardonic.) Thus all the folklore of "bitter comedians"—Mark Twain and the rest—fits in. Humor is detachment.

•

APPLY TO POETRY this sentence in *The Mayor of Casterbridge* describing Donald Farfrae's singing a Scotch ballad in the tavern: "The difference of accent, the excitability of the singer, the intense local feeling, and the seriousness with which he worked himself up to a climax, surprised this set of worthies, who were only too prone to shut up their emotions with caustic words."

•

READING HENRY JAMES'S *Washington Square* and *The Europeans,* I am curious that he invariably uses "try and—" and permits himself such an incongruous phrase as "huge morsel." I thought the Old Master was reliable in such matters. . . . By the way, this is what struck me about *The Europeans*: that anyone fictionalizing Emily Dickinson's family probably could never catch it as well as, inadvertently, James has. Old Mr. Wentworth, his attractive young son, his two daughters—one considered rather strange—their wealth and way of life: it is all but perfectly in the spirit of the Dickinsons of Amherst. And understood as only a great novelist can understand.

LITERARY NOTE-MAKING, such as this. —It is not done by one in full creative cry. Note Gide's copious example. His creative power was, I think, always very slight.

●

VACHEL LINDSAY: the Chautauqua Shelley.

●

THE ONE TIME I met Carl Van Doren the name Christopher Morley somehow came into the conversation. Van Doren said of him: "He got mellow before he got ripe."

●

ESTHER BATES spoke of a writer named Parker Fillmore who in his youth made a better than fair success with his first book, an autobiographical book. She said Robinson apprehended that Fillmore would never write another good book, because he had used himself up in the first. I told her of once reading that Auden had an uncle who said to him, "Don't write your autobiography —it's all a young poet has." . . . I don't think Spender at forty disproves this with his autobiography. For one thing, Spender has got to an age (middle) where he can use his materials directly if he chooses; for another, all his work is so fragmented— beautiful, but all to pieces—it hardly matters; (and as he himself says, all his work, in whatever form, is an autobiographical extension). . . . I can't—at forty—feel this way about my own

life; mistakenly or not, I still guard it all as poetic material. —
Later, perhaps not.

•

I HAVE ALWAYS felt a special kinship with Spender. Since first
reading his poetry I have felt there were at least elements in it
similar to my own (and I think I have even found—if this
proves anything—coincidentally similar phrases). When his
autobiography came along I found some passages in it—I
marked them but cannot at the moment recall the gist of them
—which seemed to me peculiarly true of myself. Perhaps in each
generation a writer finds a contemporary who strikes him in
this way; I don't know. I've never felt this about any other writer
except, sometimes, the poet Robert Fitzgerald.

•

SO HERE I AM, at forty-one, at last divorced from a paid job, free
to be a writer; and seldom have I felt less confidence.

•

JEFFERS is the only living poet I can think of who has evolved a
style expansive enough to manipulate all occasions, from personal to universal. He can say "Moscow" or "Munich" or
"Roosevelt" directly—just to cite one revealing characteristic.
He does not make a poetry which depends upon symbol, innu-
endo, or any kind of double-talk. Of its kind there has been

nothing successfully like it since Whitman. It is direct. It is a man speaking. Granted there are other graces and enviable ways for poetry, this way can be uniquely powerful in the hands of great talent. (Perhaps this is the reason behind my notion that Jeffers is the greatest poet now living. It isn't a notion much shared.)

●

I HEARD Margery Flack cite as a charming and functional use of specific imagery, Hammerstein's "the corn is as high as an elephant's eye." I disagree. The juxtaposition of corn and elephant is so incongruous as to be irrelevant. Even the height is lost in one's immediate, puzzled preoccupation with the picture. One sees the elephant first—the corn comes second. It is an unpleasant surprise in verse because unbelievable. —In fact, it may be cited as a sample of what one must not do.

●

FORD MADOX FORD: "But a young writer's future work will deteriorate if his first books are not full of faults and arrogance. I have found that an invariable rule." —Cf. my remarks on young poets of highly finished craftsmanship and those who fumble.

●

A WRITER MUST keep in mind, as referential, the highest achievements. There can be danger in relaxation into those smaller triumphs which can most easily be understood and enjoyed. I like, for example, to try to claim all that can be claimed for the integrity and validity of such a minor poet as Whittier, or to insist that the best work of such a secondary novelist as Tarkington needs to be assessed, or to come upon and delight in—as I have recently—the stories of Sarah Orne Jewett: their regional bouquet. And all this seems to me intrinsically right-headed. But I can see that a writer must set his sights higher. He may turn out, of course, to be a smaller writer even than the examples I have cited. All the same, the extent of his failure as an artist should be measured by incapacity and not by ignorance.

•

HERE'S A KEY word: "lonesome." I would rather write "lonesome" than "lonely." Masefield says "The lonely sea and the sky." That's British poetry. "Look down, look down that lonesome road." That's American poetry. . . . I wouldn't overstress nationalism, but it is pleasant that there are some colors peculiar to each palette. I am a nationalist in art, probably a regionalist, maybe even a localist. But one can hardly say this and hope to be understood: all three words are so often used as derogatory. And yet they are not, and almost all great art can in its sources be described by one or another of these words. One never *starts* by being universal. Impossible.

•

AS TO KEEPING one's literary sights high: somebody, perhaps Esther Bates, has said in print that Robinson read some Shake-

22

speare while at work on one or another of the Arthurian poems; and I have just been reading *King Lear* because I am trying to get back to work on my long Freydis poem. Not to "copy," nor to be encouraged or discouraged; only to remember *how* high the language can go. All this Eliot-Auden talk about poetry being a sort of game. What crap! I mean: in any sensible use of the word "game." . . . No, if one could unweave the web of *Lear* one might, however ridiculously, try to "copy"; or one might, simply, be encouraged or discouraged.

●

YEARS AGO I figured out the verse measure which most approximates contemporary American speech: it is three beats, two light and one heavy—or one heavy followed by the two light: I'm not fussy. Then I scanned some pages of verse plays by MacLeish, Maxwell Anderson, etc., where the attempt was obviously to write verse which yet would sound "natural." Sure enough, there was my measure. And that is what I have tried—as the basic measure: it isn't regular—in the Freydis poem. One frequently uses—I do, anyway—the compensatory double heavy beat. (I never can remember the names of these things.) And I, at least, can't altogether avoid the iamb. But sometimes I think one ought to stick to iambics. The strain of other measures can be too tough or, seemingly, they are frivolous; and in the long run the five-beat iambic line the most "natural" after all. *Has* blank verse been exhausted, as they say? By whom? The iamb is just a damned good brick. How it is used—that's architecture. Nobody's exhausted the brick.

SELF-DISCIPLINE. I say over and over that a writer gets nowhere without it. I smoke too much, drink too much, am too easily distracted by easier things than writing, loaf too much. And then I worry in a frustration of morning wishes crossed up by evening entertainments. Never the other way round. And I feel like a bum and get frightened—though, so far, not frightened enough. . . . And yet—and yet: I bet Katherine Lee Bates had a hell of a lot more self-discipline than Baudelaire.

●

DO YOU KNOW what actually I am doing this morning, adding these notes to my book? Actually I am putting off tackling Freydis. I make notes—other notes—for the revision and expansion of the poem. Even my wife makes notes and presents them to me: some of them very good, too. But I'm scared of it. . . . And yet I am pretty sure, as writers I suppose are always sure, that once—at last—I get in, I'll swim.

●

I THOUGHT the other day that perhaps a good many novels could be criticized for their sins of emission.

●

SOMEWHERE I have read that Hawthorne was bedeviled by the notion that he simply didn't know enough to be a novelist, and that Henry James was bedeviled the same way. I find this immensely comforting!

"THIS IS my letter to the world." (Any comment on that line? Don't be superfluous!)

●

APPARENTLY THE bigger the writer the less likely he is to originate plots in his plays or stories. Such a devilishly good playwright as Christopher Fry has recently confessed he never can think up a plot—he reads around till he finds one he can appropriate. It is noted that Shakespeare swiped the bones of his plays. And so on: lots of people—but, I think, almost always if not always, big people—from Shakespeare to Fry. There is the implication, usually, that this is odd; that it denotes a curious lack of talent in one otherwise so talented or, even, smitten by genius. What isn't noted, I think, is that such brains are consumed at infinitely harder tasks: creating things for people to say and for people to be. Creating in a sense life and simultaneously revelations of significance (which is more even than God essayed). In literature as in life, action evolves from character: not the other way around; and one can see why the kind of creative mind engaged with literature instinctively rates plotting as secondary—so much so, that kind of mind judges itself incapable of such inventions. (This needs some expansion, and some contradiction. It is not altogether true.)

●

I HAVE BEEN thinking that a basic, a philosophic rule for etiquette is this: Remember when you address another person you are addressing the center of the universe. (This is, naturally, an ex-

25

ceedingly difficult transposition for any of us to make; but perhaps it's worth trying. —Also parenthetically and by the way, I can find no reason for including the observation in a literary notebook unless I could argue the rule as specially helpful—or it should be—to writers. Maybe I could argue that.)

•

(NO PROPER PLACE to record this one either): When one's train takes a curve so that one can see, forward or back, another part of the train, that is a *peculiar pleasure.*

•

WONDERFUL REMARK in a note I had this week from William Carlos Williams. He spoke of the "disease" of wanting to write poetry, said he had been "off" poetry for many months and—he said—"I feel clean and unhappy."

•

NEVER WRITE "you who . . ."

•

THE ONLY TIME in recent years I have been really drunk—staggering drunk, whirling drunk, stumbling to one knee and vaguely up again drunk—was the night a couple of years ago in New

York that E.* and I went to see Eliot's *The Cocktail Party*. (I had first been to a real one, at Dutton's, and thought I could drink martinis as valiantly as that wonderful Russian, Nick Wreden.) Anyway, I saw, or partly saw, most of the play; and E. says I observed loudly between the acts, "This is a failure as a play because, first of all, it is a failure as poetry." Later I told this to Horace Gregory, who said, "I feel exactly the same way about it, and I saw it cold sober." S. Foster Damon taught me long ago that in poetic drama, drama and poetry are—should be—so welded that the poetry *is* the drama. I still believe it. Eliot's play has other ridiculous aspects, but certainly its fatal error is in assuming that verse can slack to such limpidity and still breathe. It don't.

•

JEFF WERNER said the other day he thought Eliot must be rated the great poet in English of the first half of the twentieth century. I said: Hardy? Yeats? Well, Jeff said, then of our era since World War I because, he said, Eliot has changed the language; other people—myself and who-all—write differently because Eliot has written. (Very probably; though I think it the duty of my generation to *try* to write as though Eliot hadn't existed: I mean—our only salvation lies in opposing him; it's the age-old, necessary revolt.) Also, I question whether later generations rate highest a poet who most profoundly influenced his time. I'm not sure that's the reason a poet is read in later generations. Jeffers? I asked Jeff. No—no, he said. Later I showed him a longish poem in the current issue of *Poetry* (Chicago); by someone named Tolson; a cryptic, allusive thing which comes supplied with pages

* Eleanor, the poet's wife. In later entries she is also referred to as "El."

of small-type notes giving sources in the Bible, Melville, and other fashionable places. (The whole thing could be a hoax, but that's always a hard problem.) Anyway, here is a thing utterly derivative—from Eliot most of all. I said: It isn't *The Waste Land*, it's the wastebasket. Jeff said: "Get out your notebook." So I have.

•

AS TO the old bull session question of how much the poet—the artist—is interested in communication. Joel, going-on-four, has a set of plastic clowns which interlock; you can make various pyramidal arrangements with them. While he was making one the other morning he was wholly absorbed: quiet, intent, unaware of the rest of the household. As soon as he had completed, he set up a yell: "Come here! Come here and see what I made!"

•

THERE IS a lot of bad writing in magazines, but none of it infuriates me as does the high-class self-conscious condescension of the quarterly critics. No doubt I underestimate their value but on the whole they are a sterile lot wedded to a few subjects and to styles of elegant, abstract jargon. The subjects change, depending on the leader of the sheep; it may alter, slowly, from Yeats to James to Kafka to Rilke—the whole herd of critics will trample back and forth over such as these for years at a time—but the picayune attitudes will not vary. Much of this in the name of the New Criticism. But the temper is not new. Goethe in his time warned a young historian against believing anything he read in the critical quarterlies. Some American writer—I forget which, but a good one—has said that if he'd espoused the wisdom to be found in such journals in *his* youth, he never would have amounted to a goddam. Oh, I don't mean to dismiss them as parasites. Even less healthy is the reaction you often see in popular writers who, though they reap their hundreds of thousands in readers and dollars, are sore as hell at their bad press and miss no chance to slay all critics as envious little people. Not so, not so. But the arrogant, typical, academic bastard who turns out the customary quarterly "Note on" this and that has a repulsive air of considering criticism—and consequently himself—much superior to mere creative work in which, hurray, the practitioners make so many errors. . . . In any case, I think the creative writer, and particularly the young creative writer, had better avoid reading such pieces. Elizabeth Bishop has printed her reaction: that after reading them, the writing of a poem seems for a long time inconceivable. Frost once murmured to me: "All these things people say —it's better [than reading them] to go dig post-holes."

●

I COMMEND to all students of prose a Foreword by Stephen Tennant to a book called *Willa Cather On Writing* (Knopf, 1949). It is so badly written in a particular way that a very important thing may be learned from it. It is written in the one-two or seesaw style: never one adjective or adjectival phrase alone, never one verb if another similar verb can be attached to it. I exaggerate; it isn't literally never—nonetheless it is so prevalent that I have marked the trick, line after line, through Mr. Tennant's twenty pages. Thus: "To write with the necessary detachment and circumspection . . . her vigour and individuality . . . the *déjà vu*

29

and the *parti pris* . . . mature and seasoned . . . the swift, benign way in which she devises and constructs a frame, a proscenium . . . she furnished and gave . . . starkly or bleakly . . . fledged around, circumscribed, and embellished . . . colour and music, verisimilitude and gay ardour . . . the drive and force . . ." and so on. I have torn these phrases from only two of Tennant's pages. Twenty pages of it make one dizzy. Even the instances where the second word or phrase does in fact enhance the meaning, potency is lost because of the unnecessary back-and-forth going on all the time. . . . I have myself sinned a great deal in this way, and the important thing which such bad writing reveals is not simply an ineffectual style, it is this: such writing arises from imprecise thinking.

•

I WONDER if one could learn to write well by fixing one badness at a time, patiently eliminating that; then on to another, and so on. One might wind up with a style in which there was nothing bad—except that there was nothing good. Still, used in moderation, *and* by a person with real talent, this method might be profitable.

•

IT IS SAID that writing can't be taught, and it is said that the most you can do is show students what *not* to do. I have been sitting here idly imagining a student who, on the basis of my remarks on Tennant's seesaw style, might worry to improve "To be or not to be."

OH, BUT ONE can be positive by illustration, too. Turn immediately from the Tennant Foreword to any of the subsequent pages of Willa Cather, and see the unhesitant march of that prose. In the context of immediate contrast, it is a revelation.

•

CLARENCE PHILBRICK said a good thing the other evening. He was talking about contemporary nature-writers for whom, Henry Beston excepted, he has no use. He compared them to Thoreau in their keeping of journals: "They report that the bobolink has arrived, but," he said, "unlike Thoreau they don't know what to *do* with the bobolink once they've got it." . . . That same evening I heard a lecture, a very good one by Professor Twadell, on the editing of contemporary dictionaries. Speaking of how the editors constantly comb current literature, Twadell excepted poetry: he said the hallmark of contemporary poetry seems to be the use of words in unaccepted ways. I thought: Yes, in ways which will have to be accounted for by dictionary editors fifty or a hundred years from now.

•

AM I ARROGANT? Very well, then: I am small, I contain multitudes.

•

SOMETIME BACK, I quoted Stevens on poetry arising from literal things. Now I have been recalling, and crossing the remark with

Stevens', how Elliot Paul once said to me that he could care little for Lovecraft's stories because there is horror enough in human experience without bringing in imaginary horrors from outside. Putting the two observations together, I can define my own limited interest in Lovecraft's kind of story; it is not real—it is antipoetic. Lovecraft himself, the Providence eccentric, fascinates me still; but I see now that his kind of mind is fundamentally perverse—finicky with the past, childish with the "made-up," antagonistic to reality and therefore to poetry.

•

SO HERE I am, at forty-one, at last divorced from a paid job, free to be a writer—and once again I have no publisher. Five books, five publishers. And I have to begin all over again. Poets can't be choosers.

•

I KNEW years ago of one man, C. A. Pearce, who was an ardent and able magazine poetry editor; but he became a publisher.

•

HOW CAN H. S. Canby write a whole book on Henry James and Mark Twain and neglect to mention (1) that James said Twain appealed only to rudimentary minds and was "a barbarian," and (2) Twain said he wouldn't read *The Bostonians* on a salary? Also, when C. devotes some pages to James's affinity to Jane

Austen—no mention of Twain's definition of a good library: Any library which does not contain the books of Jane Austen. Here's a thing I wished C. had tracked down: in Paine's life of M.T. a letter of Livy Clemens' is quoted about her being at a dinner in London where H.J. was also present (Livy, unexpectedly, liked him): was Mark—in all probability—there? If so, then the two at least once met face to face. . . . C. says Susy Clemens died of brain tumor—it was meningitis; and he misdates the publication of *The Mysterious Stranger*. There are many bad and several ungrammatical sentences in the book which make it seem a little senile. It says some good things. But it does not justify itself. H.J. and M.T. were utterly different artists—that is a simple, known fact—and the book adds nothing to everyone's perception of the point. Obviously C. must have assumed great revelations would result by placing the contrasts side by side; but not so.

●

DR. WILLIAMS said a charming thing. He read—before an audience at Brown, early in December—that famous little poem "The Red Wheelbarrow":

> so much depends
> upon
>
> a red wheel
> barrow
>
> glazed with rain
> water
>
> beside the white
> chickens.

He said a woman wrote him when the poem was first published and said, "I *like* it but what does it mean?" And Williams said he replied: "It means the same thing as the opening of Keats's *Endymion*. 'A thing of beauty is a joy forever.'" But then, Williams himself is a charming person; even at sixty-eight, seemingly wide open, boyish. When, at the beginning of the reading, he loosened his tie, said, "I'm going to be comfortable and I hope you'll be the same," one couldn't help wondering if some of the naïveté is foxy; he can't really be unconscious of the role of simple doctor-poet. Yet—and this is what matters—I see no question of the fundamental simplicity of character. For one thing, his bundle of ideas is small and rudimentary: he "hates sonnets," he wants us rid of the iamb, or certainly of iambic pentameter ("Hillyer says it can't be varied; but that's because *he* can't think of any way to vary it"); and so on; all necessary and good for him, but not the absolute gospel he thinks. It will be discovered, I think, that such ideas as Williams has he swiped from Pound; cf. the "usury" stuff at the conclusion of *Paterson*. But again this is no matter. Dudley Fitts's wife had recently said to me that she was disappointed in Williams' *Autobiography*— which I think, though it ravels toward the end, a delightful book —because "it had no philosophy of life." But I said, "Of course not: one doesn't go to Williams for that—he's an emotional catalyst, an impressionist, not at all an intellectual." The virtues of his limitations are fine ones; they make the purity of his best poems. He kodaks as he goes. Of course the poems now and then are more precise pictures (though they alone are a very difficult thing to do); for instance, the longish one about the beautiful waitress at Atlantic City—"Wait on us, wait on us." He read that, and for me it was a discovery. For most of his audience, too, I think. Many youngsters—Pembrokers, School of Design, Brown men—in the audience. How he warmed them up! How he had them almost from the moment he began! He began, by the way, by saying what I usually say: Relax—listen—don't worry about the meaning—listening to a public reading of poetry is difficult—don't work at it, etc. His voice is on the thin, boyish side; it seems to be "right" for him and the poems so that, on the whole, I'd rate him as an effective reader. (What the Jewish call "a thin tongue.") There's the fun, there's the earnestness. —Charlie Philbrick and I met him at the R.R. station. George Anderson gave a small dinner for him at the Faculty Club. The rest, faculty members. Williams talked doctoring, quite a lot. He hasn't a devoted admiration for his entire profession: thinks a lot of doctors are highway robbers. Said he couldn't have gone into surgery and been a writer: thinks surgery too demanding, too absorbing. Williams said, too, he should not like the "impersonality" of surgery, and he contrasted the real relationship between patient and M.D. He thought he'd study Greek now. He brought up Whitman's "affair" in New Orleans: was amazed when I said the original manuscript of the "Once I Pass'd Through A Populous City" poem had an all-male cast. —That is characteristic of him, a part of his seeming youthfulness: he is constantly being informed—and surprised—by little things people tell him. He was wondering if Emerson had red hair; Randall Stewart thought "sandy." —Williams himself is a medium-sized man, as size goes these days; a shade shorter than myself—perhaps about five-feet-eight; white hair, but he's mostly bald; beautiful dark eyes; the fine, seemingly extra-clean white hands of an M.D. Whole air informal, not unshy but friendly, pretty easy. El heard a girl in the audience say, "Oh, isn't he *nice*!"

Williams a complete contrast—as one would expect—to Auden, whom I met about a week ago. There's your cerebral poet, and the entire character differs from WCW's. —Auden

35

came to Providence on the same errand; Anderson, Leicester Bradner, and I met him at the station, had a (rather hurried) dinner at the Biltmore; then the reading at Pembroke. He's a fairly big fellow. around six feet I should think; is forty-five now, getting heavy; thick sandy hair, touseled; sallow face rather heavily lined. Nervous—quick movements, hurried walk. His fingernails all bitten right down, the fingers grimey. Small eyes: he's apt to watch you when you're not (apparently) watching him. Though in my case it may well have been he was trying to figure out who the hell I was. When I mentioned seeing Wallace Stevens recently, Auden said, "Are you in the insurance business, too?" And as, naturally, I went on mentioning likely subjects— our mutual friend Norman Pearson, for instance—the National Book Awards meeting (of which I shall make some notes here presently)—it was obvious I was some sort of literary joker; but either Auden had not even caught my name or, as I rather think probable, "Win Scott" meant nothing to him. In any case, he struck me as the sort of person not really interested in people. Such conversation as went on for an hour or so at dinner was casual, off the top of the mind; a little of current events, A's questions to Anderson and Bradner—polite questions—about Brown, etc. That is, mention of Pearson, for instance, led nowhere: "Oh, yes: I'm staying with him in New Haven tomorrow night." Period. We got talking about seafood—Auden thinks the best in the world is here on the northeast American coast, and I described the different but excellent lobster in Bermuda—it must be, Auden said, like the Mediterranean lobster—and I happened to speak of a specially good restaurant for it in Bermuda, in a house Tom Moore frequented (there was a lady there in his day to whom he wrote poems). "Tom Moore in Bermuda! Why, I never knew that," said Auden. "You know the lyrics are lovely." I said I thought Yeats had knocked Moore out of the way; also

36

that I remembered the long poem *Lalla Rookh*. "Oh, no, that's not good; I read it the other day. Nobody talks about Tom Moore, but the lyrics are lovely." —About my alleging his seeming disinterest in people—he's a "cool" as the saying goes—this somewhat damaged his public reading. He reads well, but he seemed —almost always—indifferent to the poetry and to the audience. A nervous trick of consulting his watch—several times—while literally in the middle of a line, and without pausing. Of course one does not know what the pressure on personality may be to have been, and since youth, the most famous and most influential poet of a generation; perhaps to be, after Eliot, the most widely known poet in English in our time; and also to be, obviously, a very brilliant and complex personality. At dinner an amusing thing happened which Auden took extremely well. Suddenly a gray-haired gent—respectable-looking; *he* may have been "in insurance"; but well oiled with liquor—stopped at our table, gripped the back of Auden's neck in one hand and the back of mine in the other. He said, "You fellers look as though you'd enjoy a good story. Have you heard the one about the feller shopping for a bra for his wife?" Auden said he had. Undeterred, the man went on, keeping his neck grips securely the whole time. "The clerk says, Do you know what size? No. Grapefruit? No. Oranges? No. Lemons? No. Eggs?—*Fried!* Howdyalikethat, huh? Well, so long, fellers. Have a good time." Throughout this, Auden grinned very patiently up at the man bending over us and came in on each "No" and on "Fried!" with a mixture of amused detachment and someone acting the part of a brother Elk. He was really very good about it. —Auden drank a couple of martinis, smoked Lucky Strikes, ate an "English" chop, a kidney, and a boiled potato.

I suppose what I'm writing here today should be called Some Memorabilia; or, You Never Know Whom the Grandchildren

37

Will Want to Read About. I'm sorry I don't seem to be writing well.

Anyway, between these two readings—about the last of December—I went to New York (back the same day) to attend the meeting of the poetry judges for the National Book Award. Present: Bill Cole, a Mr. Cameron of the publishing business, Peter Viereck, Wallace Stevens, Conrad Aiken. Absent: Selden Rodman. Cole and Cameron of course were there to conduct— and to offer whiskey. I suppose the meeting ran three to three and a half hours. As with Auden—or, as I should have said with Auden—I can record only brief and first impressions, and it's anyone's guess how trustworthy they are as accurate record. In particular, I should be guarded about Aiken; for he is—was that day—so quiet, gentle, shy. Yet if one knows him well, year in year out and in liquor, he may emerge far more definitively. As it was, the man I saw—first as he came hesitantly in the doorway —has all the presence of a seedy, disappointed, roundish, smallish, bald Sunday School superintendent. This impression, which I think is unfair—and by the way I liked him; I thought him considerate, kind, observant—was no doubt re-enforced by Stevens. It's true that Stevens, after his fourth Scotch (which he took straight), said to Aiken, "I believe that sooner or later shy people get to know each other. Take us. If you weren't shy I'd probably never have got together with you." It's true, but nevertheless the contrast was marked. Stevens is big, ruddy, talkative, assertive; one beheld the insurance executive if not the poet. S. seemed a humorous, outgoing, high-living, successful man; not one, though, to stand for any nonsense. He's seventy-two, or seventy-three. Aiken about ten years younger. Their careers have differed markedly too: Aiken much more attention when he was young than he gets now, Stevens exactly the other way. (Stevens is the enviable one in that.) I had always wanted to meet Aiken; for as a kid I read him——imitated him now and then—and still feel that he is one of the best unappreciated writers alive. —All that vague music, but there are poems that coalesce. I recall that years ago Jack Wheelwright told me he had told Aiken—characteristic of Jack's upperclass bluntness—that A. should select sharply; but A. told Jack he didn't know how to do that. —Stevens (I think, upperclass Reading, Pa.) can be blunt too. Viereck was being rather shrilly favorable toward Theodore Roethke's book, *Praise to the End!*; to get the Award, that is. I said there were charming things in it but I regretted so much of it sounded as if Ophelia wrote it just before taking off. Finally Viereck turned to Stevens and said, "Mr. Stevens, what do *you* think of Roethke's book?" Said Stevens, "It's terrible!" Also, earlier, Stevens asked me what I was doing, and I told him. "Well," he said, "you must have married a rich girl or come into an inheritance." —Viereck, I think, is a career boy; a younger and much less talented Auden —nervous, rapid, a shock of yellowish hair, much on the make in a literary sense. (He had, unaccountably, mailed me a batch of autographed magazine clips of his articles and poems a few days before. We had never met.) Not so damned bright as his reputation alleges; when Stevens asked him to say how he'd de- scribe Marianne Moore's poetry, V. wandered in the air from one cliché to another. Of course, it's not easy—pinned suddenly, like that. (Bill Cole says Stevens was baiting Viereck.) —The Award is to go to the Moore *Collected Poems*. Stevens and Aiken were a hundred percent immediately for it, V. mostly for Roethke, Rodman (by mail) largely for Roethke. I spoke for Horace Gregory's *Selected*: (1) that it was a fine book, (2) that since this new Award had hitherto been given first to Williams, then to Stevens, we ought to consider the danger, if that was the word, of pinning it repeatedly on the same generation. Stevens thought that over—came back to it once or twice. He thought this was almost undoubtedly the only chance for MM, that her book was "far and away the most outstanding," that it would rather be "ungallant" to her not to give her the Award, and that as to the age business—well, that was the way things went, the younger people would "get their chance in a few years." Aiken concurred in this. A. has, by the way, a soft, Cantabridgian (Mass.) voice: remarkably like Hillyer's. I said that of course I had nothing but respect for MM—didn't for a moment question the quality of her book, etc. And so I gave sixty percent to Horace, forty percent to MM. . . . Aiken said to Stevens: "Is it true that years ago when Witter Bynner was having a heavily patriotic phase and was late to a party where you were, you said 'We must wait for the Star-Spangled Bynner'?" S. laughed and said, "That's apochryphal. I said it, but I said it *to* Bynner." Stevens said he didn't care for Robert Lowell's book—wasn't impressed—but was impressed with Randall Jarrell's. I said I liked Jarrell's, but didn't he (S) think that in about every instance the poems went loose, weren't quite right—no matter how interesting much of the stuff may be. "Well," S. said, "he's not fastidious. But he's good—far better than your man Gregory." I could see that neither S. nor A. had any liking for G.'s poetry though neither one said anything specific about it. All these people were friendly, pleasant to be with. The little drinking—few highballs—helped. And Stevens, whose anecdotes included several drinking parties, got ruddier and practically jovial on his several "Just a quarter of an inch, Mr. Cameron" Scotches. In gray fedora and dark blue Chesterfield, he looked very handsome as he left. He had first, in the next room, made a phone call. Then he said, "I'm going to see a girl." And off he went.

I can think of odds and ends more, but this will do. Unless, later, I recall something of real or relevative importance. Frank

Merchant once said to me that I was really born to write a literary chitchat column. That wasn't nice of Frank.

•

WHEN I WAS a youngster and full of notions of the glory of being a writer, I used to mourn—I remember—what seemed to me a sad state of affairs: that, being customarily dead at the time, writers couldn't read the books written about them. And even now I would permit, if I could, Keats, Miss Dickinson, and a few others a posthumous glance so they might know what they had no inkling of: that all had been justified. But I see now that death is a blessed state for the famous, once the biographies and the studies begin. Can you imagine any writer finding even one about himself that would seem to him either accurate or fair? or that would *be*, at least, accurate in fact and surmise? The one person who would know better is, after all, cheerfully dead. He is spared anguish, bewilderment, exasperation, and mere human dumfoundment.

•

THE DARTMOUTH Eye Clinic has proved that no two people see a thing precisely the same. I have used this (three or four years ago) in a lyric—"Obdurate Change." But now I am struck with how directly this scientific discovery could be used as a line to the old doctrine of Individualism. Or, if you like, Romanticism.

•

WHEN A REPORTER the other day in New York said something

usual about the difficulty of modern poetry, Marianne Moore replied, "Why shouldn't it be work to read what it is work to write?" At once I decided it was an excellent remark. Now, a couple of weeks later, I think: It is *almost* sound. But in any case, it was a good reply. . . . Miss Moore also said that day she was not sure that her own work should be called poetry, but she didn't know, she said, what other category it would go in. An amazing woman: her humility is genuine.

•

MUCH IS SAID about the value, the necessity of solitude for the writer. I believe all of it, and at last I am able to have a great deal of time to myself. Yet this kind of life has also a danger which I think is seldom if ever commented upon, and that is that a poet's standards may relax if he is so much by himself as to have no give-and-take with other minds, creative or critical, as absorbed in the seriousness of literature as his own. To be much by one's self is to be much bemused of course with one's own thoughts; and what a short step it can be to bemusement with what is easily written. This danger is most threatening to the poetic rather than the intellectual type: the poetic in the sense of one who acts primarily via his moods and his nerves— who is not first of all a thinker; or when he thinks, he thinks via hunches. So all is as personal as his stomach's digestion or in-digestion, and he is more likely to be affected by it than to have an objective view of it. Granted that his quiet life is in most ways best for him, all he can do as to the danger is (1) now and then go seeking his peers and betters and (2) without imita-tion keep constantly in mind what are to him the touchstones of his art.

I HAVE PROMISED to be one of the judges again in *Scholastic Magazine*'s national high school poetry contest. I served last year for the first time. And I was much interested in two or three theories and revelations which, so it seemed to me, I got from the job. In the first place, evidence of imitation showed that Carl Sandburg is the most attractive poet right now [1952] for American youngsters; after Sandburg, Masters and Frost; then, noticeable touches of Robinson, Yeats, Lindsay, probably Amy Lowell or the general free verse movement of her era; and, in the traditional lyric, Frost again and Millay. There was no sign of most of the poetry which has flourished in the past quarter-century. No remarkable change—Yeats only, I think—in the list of poets I and my kind were imitating twenty-five years ago in these same *Scholastic* contests. We were then immediate heirs of an exciting renascence and so not likely, in proportion to the present day, to have groped back yet another twenty-five years to Markham, Carman, Kipling and Henry van Dyke. But the twenty-five years just past have been crowded with vital poetry: the explanation can not be that we have sagged into impotency again. So why are present-day beginners feeding on exactly the same poetic sources? Is it a teaching lag? There are ominous signs. —I don't mean I want always to discover influences in youngsters' poetry, though usually they are there; above all, I don't mean I *prefer* the latest influence to any older one. My observation is utterly simple and my question also. . . . There is another aspect to this business of influence and poetry contests which leads into a very old question: Why do the youngsters whose writing attracts prizes and attention rarely emerge as writers later on? It seemed to me I discovered at least a part of the answer. The first-prize poem was a remarkably well-managed lyric in the manner of Yeats. Nothing else in the twenty groups of poems the judges saw had its technical skill, its con-

43

trolled tone, its sophisticated polish. Take all the poems as they stood, one had to say it was the best piece of work. Derivative, yes: but so were many more. There were among them, however, poems which interested me more—poems which in their less expert manners might be coming from deeper sources. In comparison to the prizewinner, they looked—home-made. They had that flicker of promise, though. And there we get the clue. Necessarily the prizes go to the best-made work. Therefore what we cite is maturity of style, not maturity of content. The maturest of such styles is bound to be the most skillfully borrowed. The maturest of such contents will be the most personal, the stirring intimations of the process of self-discovery which is the process of maturity. The quick knack of imitation is per se probably the least healthy of signs. It is good for prizes, temporarily.

•

I CAN NOW cancel half of what the foregoing note has to say. Recently I have read the manuscripts for *this* year's *Scholastic* poetry awards, and such influence as seemed evident was pretty surely that of the Eliot-to-Auden era. No sign of the older era; or, if there was, so little that my previous curiosity was still invalidated. So what can I conclude? Nothing. . . . I read aloud some of these notes to members of the English Department at Phillips Andover one night in February, and they were incredulous of that one on the poetic influences: the boy poets at their school, they said, were most certainly Eliotish or post-Eliot. And we supposed a more sophisticated teaching level (than at the usual high school) accounted for this. . . . Perhaps this is a freak year with the *Scholastic* entrants. Or perhaps these delays of poetic acceptance really do run a quarter-century, and—

44

Click!—here it's happened. This year, the poetry I thought most impressive was a ten-page verse play which took on the meaning of life and found it tenuous, had the dry oblique style of contemporary verse, and alluded to Rilke and to Randall Jarrell. . . . I would say, to be a good scientist about all this, that I await further evidence.

●

THE NOVELIST Daphne du Maurier said in an interview this spring that Shakespeare of Stratford could not have written the plays for it is incredible that that small-town boy with a modicum of schooling could have accomplished such works of genius. This is the frequent suspicion. In fact—come to think of it—I suppose it is *the* First Cause from which all the Baconians, De-Vereists and others operate. Probably, too, my simple answer has been made; nonetheless, here it is: If education is the source of genius, why have not a thousand better-educated literary people not surpassed nor even equaled the Shakespeare plays? . . . I could go on piling up ancillary questions, but that's the central one and no anti-Shakespearian can answer it without equivocation. The burden of proof does not rest upon the Stratfordians, it rests very squarely with the opposition—and they simply cannot furnish the proof.

●

A PERSONAL RECORD. I am surrounded at the moment with anniversaries and am in a mood to make a tally. It will be a year tomorrow since I took leave of my job; I had my forty-second

45

birthday a couple of days ago. Well, I have kept this literary journal by fits and starts—which is the way I expect to keep it; and I have made notes for poems long and short, and for a number of literary essays. I have written two articles—a lyric reminiscence of Newport and a lyric criticism of *Our Town*. I have written sixteen short poems, perhaps half of them "you may say, satisfactory." I have completed (last week: and this was the thing above all I was determined to do) the rewriting of *The Dark Sister*, a poem which runs about a hundred and forty typed pages and of which I wrote a first version just fifteen years ago. I suppose I shall tinker with a word here, a line there—but to all intents and purposes that old man—that mad lady, rather—of the sea is off my shoulders forever. No longer there between me and other things—"Walpurgis," etc.—I should settle down to. I have also put together my post-*Mr. Whittier* collection of poems, about seventy pages; and that in turn I have —for the moment anyway—placed as the opening "book" of a three-hundred page manuscript drawn from the five published volumes. I have written occasional book reviews, given a few readings, had some part in poetry-awardings, and so on; have handled, spasmodically, more than my usual amount of correspondence; have read less, but more consistently in the established, though erratically: only briefly, now and then, according to plan. For whatever it's worth, I have met—generally without seeking them—a surprising number of writers. . . . Also: I have chored indoors and out, have been involved in numberless social occasions, have loafed, have wasted time. . . . As to quality, I can't judge the record; as to quantity, I'd say it's pretty good. Depends on the comparison: with Dickens? with A. E. Housman? As to *quantity*. Of course, once resigned from the literary editorship, I was assured by such diverse characters as Elliot Paul and John Holmes and I forget how many others, that

I'd need months of doing nothing before I "adjusted." Sometimes I coasted on the assurance, but sometimes I did not. I swing from glory to desperation, but seldom come to rest midway. . . . As to publication, I have no cause for optimism at all; on the contrary. The articles, book reviews, some poems—all published or about to be; but as to book publication, I'm out in the cold and the dark. First I sent, as *Scrimshaw*, the new manuscript of short poems to Macmillan. The rejection was pretty prompt: *Mr. Whittier* had sold "disappointingly" and Macmillan wanted no more of me. It was then I multiplied my stakes so arrogantly by boxing up the new poems with the earlier books, which I had cut, tinkered with, revised, rearranged, for several years; and then that I began to play my friends in New York. Bill Cole and Lucy Johnson tried me at Knopf's, then Lucy's husband Pyke Johnson at Doubleday, and then Elliot Graham at Dutton's. I've had three months of silence now from Dutton's, and with Elliot I've run out of publishing friends, I think. So a rejection from there will give me pause. (It is my notion of course that some publisher will, understandably, refuse to take on the 1932–1952 assemblage but will gamble on the first "book" by itself.) Just now I have no plan whatsoever for sending out *The Dark Sister* —which, in any event, has to have one more typing and I'm momentarily sick to death of the poem. . . . As a matter of fact, things seem to be tough all over for poetry; this is the year, as John McNulty would say, that the owls are so bad. Book costs are tough, poetry sales are worsening. One hears rumors of rejections and broken contracts. And the week to week listings of new books are a seeming proof: dreary lists of vanity-published verse, but except for a Hillyer and a Dylan Thomas, no considerable new book of poetry this whole year that I know of. I say "seeming" because other causes or coincidences may be operating with the poets themselves; the autumn may turn lavish.

47

But I rather doubt it. . . . Oh, I have also, this past year, been twice interviewed: once for the Brown undergraduate magazine, and once for *Yankee*; and I have recorded an hour or two of my poems for the Library of Congress. Everything happens except the fundamental solace of a regular publisher regularly arrived at.

•

QUESTION: Why should anyone try to write poetry? Answer: *Somebody's* got to.

•

AT HIS HOUSE the other night, Bob Stallman was ardently defending the importance of literary criticism, specifically I suppose the New Criticism. He said to me: "I don't know how it was with you, but I learned to write poetry by studying, analyzing other poems. I found out what a poem *is*." I thought: No—no—no. It was not that way with me. It was never that way with any poet. . . . I did not say so. Bob is volatile (a delightful, noisy talker) and it was easy not to get drawn into a discussion. But I should say such things. I should eschew the agreeable or the noncommital smile. . . . Bob is wondering if I'd be interested in joining the staff next year of his Writers' Conference at the University of Connecticut; so am I. John Brinnin, also there the other night, wonders if I'd take part in an E. A. Robinson reading at the YMHA, New York, if sometime it seems feasible to put one on; I said I'd feel morally obligated.

WHAT CAN ONE do but go on writing what one wants to write?
No other course is interesting.

•

THERE IS no point, really, in asking a writer which of his books
is his favorite. As soon ask a stone mason, building a stair, which
is his favorite step. The fact that he has a "special feeling" for
the one just completed signifies nothing—it's an emotional, not
a critical, judgment.

•

MARK VAN DOREN, as poet: the intellectuals' R. P. Tristram
Coffin.

•

WHEN I FIRST knew him fifteen years ago a friend of mine used
to call me "poetaster." The other night he told my wife he would
like to collect my books and other publications containing my
work and present the lot to the Yale Library. (He was wondering
how extensive and difficult a job this might be.) . . . I'm afraid
that I can't take much satisfaction from either extreme of his
views. No judgment is involved in either. Fifteen years ago he
knew nothing of my work: he knew only that I, a fellow worker
on a newspaper, wrote verse. He must have assumed it had no
value because I was alive or because he had never heard of me
or because he knew me. (Who said this?—"A dead poet is con-

sidered a great man but the man writing poetry in the next room is a damned fool.") An astonishing number of people assume they would never know a bona fide poet, and that if they do actually know a man who writes verse he cannot possibly be of importance. This attitude is such a mixture of humility and self-conceit that I despair of explaining it. But I *feel* the truth of it. This friend of mine—and he has become a close and good friend over the years—still has, I think, only scattered knowledge of my poems; he is, I suspect, impressed by certain public "recognitions"—he is taking as proof of quality the very outward incidents which never prove anything of the sort. (I don't mean to be cold about this, and I don't rule out his evident affection for me; but that alone would not suffice to explain his reaction. He is too matter-of-fact for that.) He is, incidentally, an ardent Menckenite and therefore anti-poetic. His chief delight in reading is the rather highly conscious prose: Melville, Henry Beston, and so on—the Thanksgiving Day Proclamations of the late Governor Cross of Connecticut. . . . No, it isn't quite honest to say I can't take satisfaction from his new attitude. I am pleased. I don't care if he never gets around to his project. . . . I recall—by way of postscript—that years ago I told David DeJong, a writer, about the "poetaster" label. He said he would "never forgive" anyone who had ever talked that way to him.

•

NIGHT BEFORE last I gave a reading at the John Hay Library and for the first time read a piece of *The Dark Sister*. I read from Book 3: the opening passages on Vinland and Freydis' voyage—skipped the sailors' dialogue—then F.'s soliloquy in the dunes and the page or two of further voyage. It seemed to go over, especially the soliloquy: I "had" the audience during that—you can always tell. Kappy thought it was "terrific characterization," and that from him is high praise.

•

AT THE MOMENT I seem to be in a phase of indifference about publication: no hurry about *The Dark Sister*, etc. But I doubt if I really am indifferent. I think I have my thickskin on. That manuscript of all my short stuff, so many months kicking around New York and now months of silence from Dutton's, which currently has it: all this no doubt so chills me against hope that a certain self-delusion is taking place. One always wants to be published.

•

WE WENT to Storrs a week ago to hear Dylan Thomas read: short, stocky, a fat face, thick ripple of dark hair, impressive eyes—above all, a magnificent voice: an actor's voice, controlled, varying, with dazzling range. He read some 20th century Britishers—Lawrence, Yeats, E. Sitwell, Alun Lewis ("The gradual self-effacement of the dead"), Auden; and then five or six of his own poems. There are few if any younger poets—D.T. is thirty-eight, going on—who could put their own stuff alongside most of those others without embarrassment all around. He can. Still, granting his genius, I felt more than ever the limitations innate in such word-wonder. (Cf., as I always say in this case, Swinburne.) Or perhaps more strongly it was this: that his new work adds up to little and that its most effective poems are so obviously

Yeats-shadowed. . . . I don't mean to be grudging. Probably I envy his infectious fame. He has written beautiful and magnificent things: that I believe. And I must simply remind myself it's no skin off my ass. The art is what counts. And the success of one man never—never really—never in the long run—detracts from another man's work. On the contrary; and we ought to think of ourselves as common-cause soldiers, as craftsmen in the same guild. —But there *is* human nature. Alas.

●

THOMAS SAID on the platform that night at Storrs: "Yeats is incomparably the greatest lyric poet since Shakespeare." After a pause he added, "I like to say things like that when nobody can reply. There is no question period at such exercises as these. —And I leave quickly."

●

SINCE I LAST wrote in this notebook I have typed a clean copy of *The Dark Sister*; it is at H. Holt & Co. along with all my short stuff; I have spent two weeks on Cape Cod; I have done an essay on Henry Beston's work; I am trying to write poems. I can't write—I can't write.

●

I MUST BE getting old. Young men write to me, they come to me; sometimes with manuscripts, and sometimes just to talk about the Literary Career. And I read the things and I talk to the boys or I write them letters. But I am no Wise Old Man. I always tell them to be patient, and that it's a hard life. What else can one tell them? Charlie Philbrick sighed the other day that he could use "a triumph of some kind." So could I.

●

WHEN YOU THINK that so successful and so seemingly simple a person as Whittier cried out in his old age, "O, I'm a fraud! I'm a fraud! And someday they'll find it out!"

●

IT IS A distressing thing to look over one's less-than-best work. I have a thick envelope of poems which, for a line or a phrase or an idea, I have not destroyed; I have destroyed hundreds of poems but these remaining are those that have remained without being put into any of my books. But they are all-in-all so poor—they fail in so many ways that, if I look at them, I feel that anyone capable of them must be incapable of real poetry. . . . Yet, glancing at one of those poems today I felt again a flicker of possibility rising from the single line for which I've kept the thing: "Had I touched one, then all things had touched me."

●

YOU CAN'T write your symbols *first.*

ROBERT FITZGERALD, listed in this year's Guggenheim winners as "a Catholic poet." His own phrasing, I suppose. (Fitts says that Fitzgerald is the kind of Catholic who fears the Pope has *some* Methodist leanings.) If I were a Catholic poet I think I should not so designate myself, but should rather promote a move that all other kinds of poets must be identified by their various, lesser creeds.

•

ONE REASON for keeping this kind of notebook: you can put on record the retort you couldn't think of at last night's party.

•

I HAVE BEEN reading Rolfe Humphries' translation of the *Aeneid*. Comforted, on that high scale, at how much of a long poem cannot be—need not be—poetry; and yet there need to be long poems, I still think. . . . But what's on my mind at the moment is one of the small details: I think it occurs in a passage describing Hector's body dragged around the walls: how his dragging spear scribbled in the dust. How wonderful; because there is a magnificent example of how the tiny detail functions. It is so aside from the main point, yet it is the detail which suddenly creates the picture. With it, we *see* the body and the action. (Why is it in this particular instance? I think it is because we never saw Hector dragged; most of us have never seen a body dragged, and assuredly not in the van of a chariot; but we have seen *things* dragged—swerving back and forth, skittering from side to side—and at the instant our visual memo-

54

ries stir at that tiny bit of the picture our imaginations seize the entire thing.) . . . Of course there are innumerable examples of this in literature. And I think their validity is testified by analogies in life. The other day I saw a catbird alight in a slim young maple tree which we had had put in on the south lawn last fall. Suddenly the new tree was real to me as it had not been before; not that it was not "real" before—but this was a new feeling about it. The bird alighted in the tree and the tree was *there.*

•

EDITORS: People with mistaken notions of literature and in a position to enforce them.

•

PHOTOGRAPHS OF Henry James in his middle years should be commented upon. Gone is the shy aesthete of the youthful portrait (by LaFarge?). This bearded man has a fierce look, even a bestial look. Here is perhaps—I don't know—James at his most generative. Again this man disappears in the shaven, bald, final James, the famous James—the Grand Lama.

•

IF ONE CAN hold Whitman at arm's length and judge his poetry as poetry, one has to forgive him an all but fatal lot. I have just reread, entire, his "Song of Myself." Seventy or more pages in the closely printed text I happened to pick up. The scattered, famous lines, usually of mystic self-assertion, are wonderful. But a handful only. And there are descriptive lines—horses' hoofs on cobblestones, etc.—which are beautiful concentrations. But the sprawl of the poem is debilitating. Its extreme disorder in (especially) the descriptive catalogues offends all one's senses of form. The mawkish slyness of the homosexual passages is unendearing and is a part of the air of fake one feels here and there in the poem: a barbaric yawp which half-conceals. This is not Whitman at his greatest, but it is WW at his most representative, and I feel inclined to say at the moment that ninety percent of it is bathos. . . . Oh, of course, one does forgive him. The great moments are great enough to require that. But maybe, in the long run, one has to cut him down to real size. . . . The man who wrote "Out of the Cradle—" and "When Lilacs Last—" is still bound to look like a mountain peak. Still our completest, biggest poet. And if and when the U.S. achieves a Shakespeare, Whitman will be there—like Chaucer—in his own right, on his own terms.

•

HOW WAS so great a poet as Milton possible so soon after Shakespeare? Because, I think, in Milton's major work the whole tradition differed. He did not have to bear the weight of Shakespeare because he had something wholly different to turn to: Puritanism.

•

WHITMAN IS so mixed up with his work, it is difficult to assess his poetry with the objectivity really required to assess anybody's poetry. Some months ago—but I think I have this accurately—I read a detailed account of the last of Whitman's birthday parties: the telegrammed and written tributes, the spoken tributes over the champagne in the little house on Mickle Street: all kind of fascinating and nauseating too; and it struck me that these admirers were not primarily praising a poet at all—they regarded WW as a prophet, as the declaimer of a program, as a rhetorician of brotherhood. They saluted a great personality which had revealed itself, as they believed, in certain eloquent preachments. I can't recall anything said as though the hero were an artist. The company seemed made up not of admiring critics but of loving disciples. . . . This is significant. It means that Walt's contemporary defenders promoted (primarily) not a poet but a preacher. I can imagine some of them even thinking, "It does not matter *how* he writes, but *what* he writes." We owe them, of course, the great debt of the fight for WW's eminence, but I don't doubt they messed up the literary issues a good deal. Nor is WW himself blameless in all this.

To the extent he is doctrinaire, Whitman is an impure poet. The doctrine is widespread in his book. It has nothing to do, except as limitation, with his poetic worth.

●

SINCE WRITING these paragraphs this noon I have looked up and reread that birthday record. (It was May 31, 1891.) My recollection is substantially correct. All the emphasis is upon the exponent of democracy—and at the end Whitman makes a startling speech for world democracy. The references of the guests to WW's style are pretty much what one expects: that this style is above "style" —even that this writing is above poetry. In other words, they did not think of him as a poet as we generally think of a poet as

57

a poet. All at once one of the guests stands up and praises the lyric quality of WW's greatest poems—the "Lilacs—" in particular. And who responds Yes—yes—but there is something behind that—something more than that? Mr. Whitman. At that moment alone a genuine literary judgment is offered—the one kind of judgment which ultimately must assess Whitman—and it is Whitman himself who dismisses it as a minor observation. . . . Whitman, aged, sick, vain as he is, nonetheless makes clear his perfect consciousness of a role: he has "uttered" (perhaps not his word) *Leaves of Grass* to utter everything; even he does not wholly comprehend it, etc., etc. This is a would-be prophet speaking, perhaps a would-be messiah. Did Whitman want to be the messiah of homosexuality?—The question sounds ridiculous; but is it? He never *said* as much, and therefore all the "mystery," the "something beyond that," the air of evasiveness, of not coming to terms. But the evidence of his profoundest dream is blatant in the poetry. You find it scattered everywhere, you find it concentrated in "Calamus": the section WW himself said meant more than all the others. And what, on the evidence of the poetry, does Whitman mean by "manly attachment," "the secret of my nights and days," and "the need of comrades."? He means: men naked, playing together; men sleeping, embraced together; men tongueing each others' bodies, caressing each others' bodies full-length, and achieving emissions. I put this all plainly, avoiding the actual quotations, to avoid the slight fogginess of meaning which W's actual language usually contrives. But no adult can read these passages without realizing that they mean exactly the blunt things I say here they mean. . . . I know it begins to seem tiresome, and perhaps sophomoric, to talk about Whitman's sex. But though there has been a lot of discussion of it, much of that discussion has been idiotic or dishonest; much of it, at least, beside the point. What besides personal prejudices are so many students of WW hindered by? Lack of "facts." But the *truth* about Whitman is in the poetry: he celebrates it as daringly as he can, and he points to it. (See Ludwig Lewisohn on this. Twenty years ago L. crashed right into the heart of the matter: Whitman was a homosexual, said L., and a homosexual of the most aggressive kind.) . . . Well, I think the final findings will go something like this: Whitman was a mamma's boy. Somewhere near his thirtieth year, and probably on the New Orleans trip, he had a sexual awakening: he knew, at last, what he was and what he desired. Then he wrote his own real work at last. The work contains many things, but in WW's mind its core was his kind of sexuality. He did not espouse it in specific terms, but he wagered he would be understood by men with similar desires. (Oh, he denied the charge when Symonds wrote him the question direct; he lied about having women and children; he dissembled all around the homosexual question—but, but: he had a mask to maintain, a secret to keep.) And, finally, yes: I think he meant to be a recruiter for his cause. . . . Comradeship: democracy: sure—but what Whitman passionately loved was young men's bodies. I doubt if he ever had a woman; if he had, I'm sure it was for him a disillusioning experience: "cold mutton," as Oscar Wilde found it. Note in the poems how much less vivid the naked woman passages are than those of the naked man: a sop thrown in; and how quickly most of them turn the woman to her role as mother—not fondling over her role as sexual companion. . . . Yes, I think WW achieved one thing (among others) he wanted to: isn't he, after all, the great poet of homosexuality? This was his deepest interest: not poetry per se. And sublimated, it made his greatest poem—"When Lilacs Last In the Dooryard Bloom'd."

AMONG THE guests at that 1891 birthday dinner of Whitman's were a Miss Clark and a Miss Porter, otherwise unidentified. But these must have been the Browning editors. I have met and talked with Miss Porter. Twenty or more years ago, Foster Damon took me as his guest to meetings of the New England Poetry Club, and Miss Porter—Charlotte Endymion Porter—was then a very old lady, her white hair bound by a baby-blue ribbon. I can't recall anything else about her except I had been told she had been—ten or fifteen years before I met her—among the most vehement opponents of Amy Lowell and "the new poetry." When, in a N.E. Poetry Club row, Amy hissed, "Cats!" at her triumphant opponents headed by Josephine Preston Peabody, it was Charlotte Endymion who cried, "Anyway, we're not fat cats!" . . . I wish I'd known Miss P. had been to Mickle Street when WW was there. She must be dead these many years. But then, though it still meets, so is the Poetry Club. . . . All poetry clubs are stupid; an embarrassment, a waste of time. Their odor of unadmitted mediocrity is stifling. What can a poetry club accomplish? Nothing but the exhibitionism of the meagerly talented and the untalented. And whenever such organizations seek to influence contemporary poetry, they invariably boost the stale reactionary. From what I've read of it, the Poetry Society of America, being the biggest of them all, is the biggest example of what I'm saying. Such clubs are founded on the ridiculous notion that prayer is bettered by prayer-meetings. . . . See Robinson's last good work, *Amaranth*. Which, I suddenly remember, is also admired by Robert Hillyer—current prexy of the Poetry Society of America. Hillyer is a real poet and, according to his lights, for the right reasons; but he has gotten plastered over, since he gave up liquor and attacked Pound et al., with all the other peoples' wrong reasons. . . . Hillyer is as charming a man as I've ever known. And he is a scholar and intellectual profounder than many a "modernist." By conviction he is a traditionalist. He has done some lovely work and is not to be confused, as practically always he is confused, with the talentless hordes who can do nothing but copy outworn techniques and attitudes. He has his smoothness, his politeness, his goddamned impeccable taste. These make for a nice poetry. . . . I have heard him scorn Jeffers; heard him say, "I hate every line Hart Crane ever wrote"; seen him dash down a Sunday book review praising Auden for bringing back the rhymed couplet: "When," cried Robert, "am I ever going to be given credit for anything I've done!" He had a while before published *A Letter to Robert Frost, and Others.* . . . Hillyer has no use for Hopkins and reveres Robert Bridges. I think Bridges a dull dog who will be remembered if at all as Hopkins' bewildered friend and first editor. —So there we are. But RH is a delightful person to be with; has always been a kind friend to me, and sometimes voluntarily a helpful one.

●

I WONDER if Charlotte Endymion Porter aforesaid is the only person I've ever met who actually saw and talked to Whitman. I don't know. I had a friend (Dr. Koopman) who had shaken hands with Emerson; and K. and one or two other people I've known—Senator Green—met Mark Twain. Mrs. Elliott, whom I talked to in her nineties in Newport, had in her youth gone into a London dinner on the arm of Robert Browning. It is still possible for a young man—I see by the papers that rising politicians in their forties are "young men"—to be only one handshake away from great and famous people who seem remotely far in the past. After all, Mrs. Elliott's father—Samuel Gridley

Howe—arrived in Greece just after Byron's death and bought Byron's helmet, I think, at some sort of auction. Mrs. E. had Byron's Greek helmet in the house. . . . I am an antiquarian at least in this: I like old people, I like that sense of touching at near hand extraordinary lengths into the past. I like graveyards, too.

•

ABOUT WHITMAN, though: Is there a more touching sight in the literary history of the U.S. than Walt shuffling along the streets of Camden, on his arm a basket of his books for sale—and the righteous mothers of Camden drawing their children out of the way of "the dirty old man."

•

MY ROBINSON anniversary [22 August]. Twenty-three years ago today I invaded the Veltin Studio at Peterborough and first met EAR. I always think of it.

•

WE WENT the other day to see the new movie version of *Robin Hood*. It was fun. And it was restful. All the villains are black characters; Robin and all the good characters are thoroughly white. Of course this is contrary to the greatest literature; but, as I say, how restful for a change. . . . I suppose most "popular literature" bases itself on this oversimplicity; the current historical novels, for example, which sell so well. I don't know, for I never get around to reading any of them. . . . In *Robin Hood*, by the way, Friar Tuck has intimations of a great characterization. Had he only been touched by a Shakespeare or a Dickens, his Falstaffian or Pickwickian potentialities would have flowered.

●

"THE ASSISTED gold of her hair." (I think the phrase is Dorothy Parker's.) One likes it not only for the wit of the fact but also for the unexpected justaposition of the noun with that adjective. Such surprises are always delightful. And don't they often occur in just this way?—a word ("gold") romanticized with its many associations given a new strength by a comparatively prosaic ("assisted") adjective.

●

IT IS TRUE: the arts begin all over again in each child. Susan (two) responds at once to music by "dancing." Joel (going-on-five) is now occasionally rhyming: usually it's a nonsense word he makes up to match the sound of a real word he has said, but he tries to match. More interesting, perhaps, is J.'s occasional attempt at work-song: he chants along, with unmistakable rhythms, or sing-song, telling about things recently seen or done. He is a primitive. . . . A year or more ago J. did a good deal of painting, which consisted of swashing various colors on paper; these were often interesting both in "accidental" design and combination of colors. Now I notice that when he does paint—not so often—he is trying to be representational: to draw a house, etc. It's nowhere near so interesting. (A year of nursery school perhaps had something to do with it.) . . . All the arts are innate; all are justified.

WHY DO Conrad Aiken's books so frequently disappoint one when one rereads them? I think it is because one remembers their intentions, which are always superbly intelligent, and forgets their performances, which a romantic emotionalism diffuses. Those novels and short stories are so good—if only they were a bit better: they are already superior to most. Those poems— there are so many on the verge of memorability, but so few that really harden in the mind. . . . I think one admires the man, respects him, thinks of him with some excitement, because unlike most writers he is full of intimations of genius; but look, and the genius is not wholly realized. Is it because a literary veil hovers between him and the real thing? that he is a shade too thoughtful of manner, and the manner is a montage of others'? . . . His new book, *Ushant*, may be his freest and best. That and a few poems.

•

I SEE THAT Leslie Stephen—Victorian writer; father of V. Woolf —confessed a "'latent conviction" that he was "an imposter" and would be found out. Cf. Whittier's "'fraud" exclamation.

•

THE PAST couple of weeks have been pleasant in this way: half a dozen magazines appearing with poems and reviews of mine; requests for poems in an anthology (Humphries); article done for Winterich on poets and publishers, and he very pleased; some new and promising poetry begun; request for autobiographical piece for a good reference book (*Twentieth Century*

Authors, Supplement); John Brinnin to see me about being speaker at a Robinson Memorial in NYC this winter; etc. Yet how much more easily I am depressed than elated: this morning *Harper's Magazine* returned the Beston essay. Now of course they would. It doesn't in the least resemble anything they ever publish. Sending it to them was the longest elimination-shot imaginable. But I am nonetheless annoyed and blue about it. Ridiculous, but it's so. . . . Of course, over and above and beyond all this is the interminable silence (more than five months) of H. Holt & Co. on *The Dark Sister.* For the sake of the record I may write that all out when it has an ending. . . . I should add, for the record, that depressions over rejections are usually short-lived with me. A few hours, a day, and I'm arrogant once more. But while they do last, I am liable to a feeling of fatigue and to an inability to write. . . . Actually I've had a lively autumn and ought to have a warm feeling of accomplishment. But one never has.

●

NO: ONE HAS a warm feeling of accomplishment over the poem as it is (perhaps) in process; (I mean—there are so many things going on in process, this is hard to tell); certainly over the poem as it is just finished. Then comes the cooling-off. The doubts sometimes arise. The old question of the difference between what I first imagined and what I was able, less well, to accomplish. Finally: the poem won't do and is chucked out; or, the poem will do and that's that. It is for other people to be moved. Myself sometimes in a public reading; if so, usually for private reasons —for a resurgence of the sources of the poem; not as the audience, if it is moved, is moved.

THERE ARE two kinds of poetry. One, the kind represented by Crane's line: "The seal's wide spindrift gaze toward paradise." The other represented by Robinson's: "And he was all alone there when he died." One is a magic gesture of language, the other a commentary on human life so concentrated as to give off considerable pressure. The greatest poets combine the two: Shakespeare frequently; Robinson himself now and then. If I have to choose, I choose the second: I go, in other words, for Wordsworth, for Hardy, in preference to Poe, to Rimbaud. . . . This is all an over-simplification, I know; but I think the flat assertion of the two kinds indicates two very great touchstones.

•

JUST A FEW minutes ago I thought the wood fire I had just built in the stove here in my hut had gone out; that I had logged it up too fast and smothered the kindling. But I poked the sticks together and they have come on, after all.

•

LONG TIME no enter, as the monk said.

•

I THINK I may seriously announce the origin of Henry James's "mature" style. (1) "Under the impression that your peregrinations in this metropolis have not as yet been extensive, and that you might have some difficulty in penetrating the arcana of the

Modern Babylon in the direction of the City Road—in short, that you might lose yourself—I shall be happy to call this evening, and install you in the knowledge of the nearest way." (2) "Take him for all in all, we ne'er shall—in short, make the acquaintance, probably, of anybody else possessing, at his time of life, the same legs for gaiters, and able to read the same description of print, without spectacles." And (3) "We are very sorry to lose the benefit of his advice—or, as my father would say, to be deprived, to a certain extent, of the concomitant advantages, whatever they may be, resulting from his skill, such as it is, and his professional attendance, in so far as it may be so considered." The (1) and (2) are Mr. Micawber talking in *David Copperfield*, and (3) is Dickens per se imitating, as he says, his Micawber-original. . . . This should be researched further. I haven't, in fact, been rereading *Copperfield*, but have taken these quotations from Edgar Johnson's new biography of Dickens. But I submit this evidence, re James, is impressive.

•

DICKEN'S OWN style employs with amazing constancy the speech-making device of repetition; repetition of word, of phrase-structure—over and over again, pound—pound—pound. It's unpleasant because it is so frequent and so obvious. I don't mean to reduce Dickens to this—and again I haven't been rereading him: just reading Johnson's volumes. I would add, offhand, the repetitive device seems to be employed with particular virulence in Dickens' later novels. But Johnson, less impressive as critic than as biographer, makes only a one-phrase mention of the trick. . . . I must read the later novels. Like many, I precociously read Dickens when I was eleven, twelve, thirteen—in there somewhere; by which I mean of course I read *Pickwick, Copperfield, Oliver Twist, Christmas Carol, Tale of Two Cities*; but not *Great Expectations, Hard Times, Bleak House*. Nor have I yet. I've reread *Pickwick* happily enough, but once when I tried *Oliver Twist* I was dismayed and gave it up. Esther Bates said the other night she was reading *Bleak House* for the first time and, she said, "it's greater than Dostoevsky."

●

AUDEN CAME in to an Eighth Street bookshop the other day, scuttled along the lending library section and borrowed a couple of murder mysteries. . . . One must remember that seeing him is, so far as we know, the equivalent of seeing Tennyson stride into a London bookshop in 1853.

●

THE APALLING politics that seem to go on in NYC—now as ever, I suppose—in literary circles; specifically the poetic. The sucking-up to editors and anthologists, the behind-scenes plots to put over this one or that, the homosexual links, the reputable houses publishing books of poems paid for by such authors as can afford it; and so on. So much maneuvering! I said to H. G.: "But don't all these people see that all this activity is nothing? That the only thing that lasts, the only thing that counts, is the work itself, well done?" He smiled patiently at me as he does whenever, I suppose, he thinks I am both correct and naive. "That," says Horace, "isn't what they want. They want power." "But it doesn't make sense." "No."

68

ABOUT DICKENS—I like Robinson's phrase on him: "A boiling-over genius." It concentrates D.'s enormous vitality and the waste. But I suppose you couldn't have one without the other. Melville said—I was just reading this last night—that genius is full of trash.

●

ADD: CHARMING things said by writers. Arthur Miller is quoted in an interview this weekend as saying that when people praise his new play he feels like saying, "But you should have seen it before it was written!"

●

I AM READING Van Wyck Brook's *The Writer In America*—in simple, a defense of the U.S. tradition. As the Concord farmer said when he returned Emerson's copy of Plato: He has a lot of my ideas in that book.

●

I WISH I could psychoanalyze the contempt literary people express for work they esteem inferior. How a kind of *moral condemnation* is made of persons whose talents are small. I was going to say the response is a curious one, but certainly it is not curious in any sense of rarity. We all do it, almost reflexively; but some are much more violent than others. I mean, of course, the loud, "God, Jones stinks!" when the critic thinks Jones's poems are poor. Jones writes, one supposes, as best he can. His poems may indeed stink. But does Jones? Really? Why this contempt for him? Why this anger at him? —Well, my guess is that such emotions are not precisely what is operating; that what the critic is really saying is, "See how rigorous, intelligent, informed, uncompromising, superior, my standards are!" And I would further guess that the more vehemently he expresses his substitute for this declaration, the more insecure he is in his standards or, it may be, in his own creative work; or in both. Most probably in his own creative work for, thinking it over, it seems to me such harsh denunciations occur usually in the conversation of writers. Often it is much more famous writers (than themselves) who, they perceive, stink. Often it is very young, unpublished writers who are most violent in these perceptions. And so on. There are, I'm sure, multiple ramifications. But in any case I think they have little to do with Jones.

•

AS WRITERS get older most of us develop considerable interest in unappreciated writers.

•

LAWRANCE THOMPSON told me the other night in New York that he is discouraged from doing a "life" of Robinson. He says the family have a nice EAR portrait in mind and that it isn't to be violated by truth. Years ago Frost told me that there was trouble between EAR and his brother Herman over Herman's wife; as Frost told it—Herman ordered EA out of the house,

70

and it was then EA quitted Gardiner, Maine. I asked Thompson if this were the story, and he said positively, Yes—it is. . . . Walter Abel, the actor (and a great Robinson fan), was standing near us, and he wanted to know what if anything anyone knew about Robinson's sex life. Thompson said that an old friend of EAR's—I'm sorry I can't recall which one—but I think Ridgely Torrence—[said,] "I could show you the whorehouse."

●

THIS ISN'T a literary note, but it probably illustrates the simple ways in which my mind operates. The other night, thinking of some recent deaths and some warning illnesses among members of the [Providence] *Journal* staff, I thought how few years there will be before many of the people I have long known there will be gone. And I thought too, of course, of the replacements—the new people whom I don't know and probably shan't ever. And of how steadily the reasons for my going into the *Journal* building are bound to dwindle. Then suddenly I saw the analogy with life itself: how lonely very old people can be—the younger, newer people, the replacements, are not the same. Not go into the *Journal* building: not go on living. For the first time I felt, and so perceived, how one can become reconciled to death. — There is no party when everyone you knew has departed; so why stay? . . . This does not offer any reconcilement for one at twenty or forty.

●

POETRY IS always "in a bad way." At any given time in the history of the English language perhaps half a dozen people are writing poetry; or three; or even, now and then, only one. The past is easy to see. We do not have to labor to know that Burns and Blake and Wordsworth and Shelley and Keats are the names that count in one particular run of (is it?) seventy-five years; we do not have to wade about in the morass of "poetry" that went on around them. Any present is a confusion: full of so much "poetry" that nobody certainly knows which is the poetry; and so in any time one critic or more will proclaim (often as good a critic as Edmund Wilson) that poetry is "in a bad way" and "done for." History alone should better instruct such critics.

●

I SUPPOSE the hypocrisy of conventional magazines is so stupid as to be unconscious. Case in point: E. E. Cummings has been giving some lectures at Harvard, and the *Atlantic* has published a couple of them. Why? Well, because Cummings' is a big name. How has Cummings' become a big name? By writing poetry. Has the *Atlantic* ever published Mr. Cummings' poetry?—Not that I'm aware. . . . E. says of course it's simple: it is, she says, mere illustration of respect for success—no matter in what field. I realize it is in a way a small matter and a comic matter. Yet I take it seriously and a little angrily. It seems to me so perfect a specimen of the inadequacy of editorial brains, courage, and morals. Cummings, thank God, is no more respectable than he ever was. But, 30 years after his beginnings, he receives the *Atlantic*'s recognition (first confirmed of course by Harvard).

INSTRUCTION FOR reading a poem aloud to an audience: You must read as if you were then and there creating it—effortlessly but with complete absorption—and, therefore, as if the audience were hearing it for the first time. (This last is of course often literally so; but it's a good "as if" in any case.) . . . I am, apparently, an uneven, unreliable, but sometimes very effective reader of my own work. I am sure I learned at least one thing about such reading during the five years I did news broadcasting: that is—simply—you must be interested in what you are reading. Not even *seem* interested: you must *be* interested; (and this, for the moment of any one news item, is perfectly possible). All graces don't necessarily follow after this—but it is step number one.

●

GERTRUDE STEIN's writings: mostly crap, but so is fertilizer.

●

I AM HAUNTED lately by a sort of Piet Mondrian painting; I mean, made up in my own mind—the vision of verticals and horizontals, black, straight, boxing one another, with here and there the severe commentary, but charming, of a block of red or yellow or blue. And the reason I'm obsessed with this is the wonder if a poem could not be written that would feel like such a painting. The economy. The purity. Objectivity. No clutter. No "personality" save in the most indirect way. An abstracted grace.

ONE SUFFERS a kind of fatigue with repeated rejections. Still, I have started a new long poem. (I think.) Yesterday. —This business of writing what nobody wants.

•

MAUD GONNE died a week or so ago in Dublin; at eighty-seven or eighty-eight. I am reminded of a theory I have that Yeats really made her a part of his mythology—his efficacious system; that he did not in fact have a lifelong love for her. She was *his* private substitute for The Virgin. The beautiful woman unpossessed has been, time out of mind, good stuff for poetry. Yeats knew that as well as anybody, and his brainless but marvelous instincts guided him from there on. He couldn't make her Mrs. Yeats but he could make her immortal. . . . Who got the best of that bargain?

•

ALMOST ALL playwrights are no more than librettists. They provide a skeleton of speech which, embodied in players and action and tongue, can upon the stage be one way or another a moving experience. But scarcely one playwright in a century is capable of writing anything which is intrinsically interesting. It can be argued that they should not: that a play is indeed an incomplete thing until so embodied—is meant to function in just that way. And surely most of even the best plays operate in that fashion and no higher. But I would answer that the greatest plays— Shakespeare's to Shaw's—ARE the greatest plays by virtue of the same richness in language and thought which is necessary

74

to great literature. That's a simple fact which you can't get around. . . . The proportion of enduring plays to the number of all plays written seems less than that of poems to all poems, novels to all novels. Why is this? There are so many questions here. Why is it that greatly talented writers in other fields customarily fail if they try the theater? Why is it that the most talented of any era's playwrights are all the same incapable of creating things of lasting interest? The rare great man arises and does this—yes; but he is so rare that it seems as though he does it despite the requirements of playwriting. . . . Well, it may be argued that playwriting is the very highest of the literary arts: that its peaks are attainable only to the vastest poets—therefore the more numerous failures. But then why aren't the failures, in this highest sense, more crashing? No: the failures (again, from this point of view) include the most successful playwrights of our time. They are skilled. They have remarkable gifts for the typical phrase, the characteristic banality, and they can arrange these "truths" in comic or touching ways upon the stage. Yet these skills lie largely in the editorial and reportorial area: they cannot extend themselves, only their kind varying somewhat from generation to generation, into another era. They are timely and they die. . . . I don't believe the average playwright is less talented than the average novelist or poet. I think he must work in a medium which so insists upon the immediate declaration and the immediate response that he is forced to a shallow simplicity; at best, his story may reverberate within itself but not beyond itself. Therefore the play is a type, a specimen, but not lastingly a living thing. . . . From actors to stagehands, the play is at the mercy of so many forces outside itself. Unlike a poem or a novel, a play *must not be* an entity. It is the apotheosis of notation. . . . Do not bombard me with exceptions: I am aware of them. All are works of lords of language. (And though some

75

are revived, many are not, and none at any time makes the record-breaking Broadway run.) . . . If I am wrong about all this, it may be that I have too hastily guessed the proportion: that all I say here is no more significant than if I judged poetry and novels by the "average" at any time.

●

I HAVE JUST been reading Joseph Hone's *Life of George Moore.* It contains (for no apparent good reason) a penultimate chapter of reminiscences by Moore's cook, and then a critical chapter (by someone whose name I forget) assessing Moore's work. And I found myself dreaming up a plot for a pathetic short story— or rather, only the touching, essential moment in the story: famous novelist's cook piously reads the big fat volume about her late master, because she was deeply devoted to him; she gazes too with wondering pride at the chapter of her own words; finally she comes to the critique, but try as she will she cannot make headway in it, and she gives it up—but she goes patiently through it, underlining in pencil the name "Moore" wherever it occurs. . . . I recall Padraic Colum's exclamation. George Potter, who told me about it, ran into Colum on the train one day some years ago, and they talked all the way to New York. Potter brought up George Moore's name. "Jarge Moore! Jarge Moore!" exclaimed Colum: "Ohhh—a dirrrty man was Jarge Moore!"

●

WE WENT last night to hear Dylan Thomas again—at Storrs, same place as a year ago. I am right: that rhetoric is beginning to seem windy. What at first seemed powerful and inventive begins to wear out as whimsical. I don't say every poem: but most of them, and the characteristics of his poetry. Any poet these days who has even one string to his bow seems a great poet, and none has a stronger string than D.T. But, ah, the increasing deliberation of his fine frenzy. He gave, with that marvelous voice, a fine performance; a little tired, as though the voice were too accustomed to itself and so a little weary of itself. He opened, by the way, with an amusing prose skit of British authors as visiting lecturers in America; the poets "dollar-mad nightingales, myself among them, bawling the Welsh." —Something of that sort. He had the crowd in an uproar. . . . I spoke not long ago to John Brinnin about Thomas' apparent paucity of output in recent years. "Well," said John, "he's been in kind of a mess these past two or three years. Of course—he's always in a kind of a mess."

●

I NOTE THAT Yeats quotes with approval Balzac's phrase for critics: "barren rascals."

●

HOW TO BE—when all is said and done—an immortal poet: Get born that way.

●

FOSTER DAMON used to say, "The best poems are those you get out of bed to write."

THE DOG AMONG THE RILLS

For My Friend Dick

There's a groundhog in my field.
I've only seen its head yet.
Richard Eberhart need not yield—
My animal isn't dead yet.

To Mr. A.

Our poems keep separate domains
However fame befalls.
Sir, you write yours with your brains
And I mine with my balls.

The Double Life

Whenever in the fulsomeness of his fame
Mr. Oscar Williams completes a poem, he's
Likely to smite his forehead and exclaim
"There's one for the anthologies!"

The Usual

Some poets with long-tried temerity
Sat worrying over their posterity,
Unaware as the years went flitting on
'Twas only what they were sitting on.

Autobiography

This hare and tortoise race I've been assigned
I hardly can complain of, though it wears.
It isn't being the tortoise that I mind,
It's that there are so goddam many hares.

Poetry and Prose

O my luve is like a red, red rose,
And I took her out to the barn
And fucked till it shook her bones.
—Both versions by Robert Burns.

On the Posthumous Award to Harold T. Pulsifer of the New England Poetry Club's Golden Rose

Ask me no more where June bestows
New England Poetry's Golden Rose.
This year appropriately gave
That scentless burden to a grave.

Hurrah!

Madam, your little boy has
Bat ears;
And, Madam, some of my poems are
Cock-eyed;
But we had 'em—
Didn't we!

Unquote

"What is mind and what is bird
That the grave is their last word?"
(Lincoln Fitzell out on t'ird.)

Au Revoir

I've often seen a purple poet
And now I'd rather see none.
But I'll confess, lest you don't know it.
Alas! I used to be one.

Restricitve Adjective

Now he is old they keep giving
Every prize—and they love to bestow it.
"Foremost living American poet."
He says, "I must get rid of that 'living'."

•

SOMEONE OUGHT to write a novel about librarians; or a librarian. The officious male at the head of the staff; the nervous, sex-starved females on the staff—not tough enough to be school teachers, not juicy enough to be wives and mothers, not bright enough even to care for first-rate books. And yet itchy. There's always one—or two—on any sizable staff who are rather pretty; a little dimly so, faded so, but it's there. Brad Swan used to tell me he could get feeling powerfully horny just loafing about in library stacks; I recognized the feeling. It comes perhaps from the combination of quietness, one's youth, and a vibration of repression in the air. . . . Usually the head librarian is alleged to be sexually dangerous: he is rumored (1) to pat bottoms, (2) to give promotions on a sexual basis, and (3) to have a mistress on the staff; any, sometimes all, of these things. He is himself customarily a fussy, officious, dictatorial boss; and often rather an able man in his field. Like the women, he strikes one as not caring greatly for books save as commodities which inspire fascinating problems of shelving. He has "departments" in his regime, and his great passion really is the power of directing and assuaging departments. Out among men he inclines to be a bit racy—very self-consciously, because he really is an immature prurient. On solemner occasions he is given to talking pridefully of public service because, in fact, he hates the public. He is by far the best paid employee in the place: except for him, the whole staff is poorly paid; he is a little king within those walls and, in most communities, one of the better-known citizens. He is very vain since he has no genuine sense of humor. . . . Such a novel would be the damnedest mixture of shallowness, goodwill, hard work, dimwittedness, mired sexuality, misguided and embittered lives, semi-poverty, etc., etc. No novelist anxious for his sales will ever publish such a book.

●

IN THIS COUNTRY in this time women are the great majority of the artist's audience: for the poet, the musician—well, everybody knows the list. And women—a great many women—are attracted to the artist as man; they love him, they want to marry him; sometimes several in a row take turns (with some overlapping) marrying even one artist. He arouses the maternal in them and a temporary, uncharacteristic lust for an irregular, extracurricular, insecure, and remarked-upon life. But of course such lust doesn't last and furthermore the maternal instinct includes the dictatorial. In short, I suspect women are antipathetic to the artist; once they are involved with him they resent a preoccupation that no other type of man save the scientist has. Even the biggest tycoon defers at home to Mama; and with rare, dedicated exceptions, your Businessman is not really heart and soul in his work —look at how eagerly he escapes it. No, the artist is an altogether different bug. Women run from being fascinated to being repelled by him. They won't cease doing this, either, for he is a challenge to their authority.

NO DOUBT there is much more to be said about women and artists and women versus artists. Of course there are exceptions to what I have said—most of them, though, wives of artists whose importance (whether lasting or imagined) gains recognition; then there ensues reflected glory. In any case: I think the multiple marriages in the artist class relate directly to what I have been saying. The woman is attracted and then disappointed. The man seeks a relationship contiguous with his work, yet repeatedly discovers the relationship is an interference. He wants protection but he doesn't want direction; and as Robert Frost once remarked in an entirely different context, the two go together. . . . And I should say that little enough of this is autobiographical; I have no complaints.

●

I AM FOND of reading biography, particularly literary biography, and I am mutilating myself of late with what I fancy the reason for such fondness can be. Vicarious experience, of course. You take a failure of a writer or the type who in his lifelong ambition to *be* a writer has confused the ambition with the ability; and when such as he reads the biographies he experiences the illusion of experience. Thus and thus, he can say to himself, it is with me; till, toward the last, he can even feel how it's going to be to bask as a Grand Old Man of Letters. Biography can chronicle the glamour of attainment and, since it's in retrospect, the glamour of early (temporary) failure and neglect; it can record very little of the real business—the blank agony of writing, of trying to write, week in and week out. We may read that Conrad would stare helplessly for days at his study wall: the fact is comforting, but the actual depression of that experience is not conveyed. . . .

"WHAT ADVICE do you have, Mr. Robinson," I said on first meeting EAR, when I was nineteen, "for a young man who wants to be a poet?" "Well," he said, "if you've got yourself in that trap there's nothing I or anybody else can say to help you." I thought —then—"trap" was an odd word for him to use. For all I saw in the rockingchair before me was a figure glamorous with achievement and a general acknowledgment of it. . . . I know much more about R's life now, much more about the lives of other writers; a hell of a lot more—but with no certainty as to its significance—about my own.

•

I'M TRYING in my just-started long poem to move a step over, technically, from the verse of *The Dark Sister*. In that poem I was intent on having the triple, one heavy, two light, foot ($/ \smile \smile$) the basic, the most recurrent foot; the lines themselves vary a good deal. But in "The Brewing of the Heart" (which I wish I could get on with, instead of writing these notes) I'm still standing by that foot as the basic, but governing the individual line by five stresses. The attempt, thus, is to tighten up somewhere between the freer flow of the *Sister* and the exactitudes of blank verse. The point of course is to approach "natural speech." Two two apparent difficulties are: (1) not to slip over into blank verse and (2) not to pad the line to avoid blank verse. The variation of the number of light syllables per line—that is, the variation of other "feet" around whatever that DAH-dah-dah is called (I can never remember)—is of course constant and necessary. If one did the thing exactly one would be farther than blank verse from any illusion of "natural speech." . . . All this I think will be difficult to do well; I thought it might benefit me to

83

set myself a more exacting job of versification. . . . With eighty or ninety opening lines on paper my worries are something else again: Does this *need* to be verse? Is its light, naturalistic tone antipathetic to poetry? Will it rise and justify itself? Etc., etc., etc.

•

YEATS SAYS somewhere that now and again a young poet will return to the sonnet to tighten up his style. Alas, think of the young poets who have in the process merely loosened up the sonnet.

•

LAST EVENING E. and I went to Storrs and heard Katherine Anne Porter talk (to the Writers' Conference) on "the artist as a human being" and then a reading of his poems by William Jay Smith—a nice young man. We met and talked briefly with them both, and afterwards Bob and Virginia Stallman had E. and me to their house along with Miss P.—just the five of us. We drank gin and quinine. . . . At the conclusion of her speech, a boy had rushed in with a box of pink carnations for Miss P. and these she was examining in the Stallman's kitchen as E. and I walked in. "Who sent them to you?" said Bob. "Two *ladies* in the course. Oh—oh: it shouldn't happen to a dog!" (This with a merry air of dismay.) . . . She is fifty-nine, more gone in the skin than her glamorous photos led me to expect; but for all that an attractive woman. An extraordinary combination of Southern belle and intelligent woman. A curious affectation of an ever so slight French accent in her public talk; but as the gin and quinine evening developed, the "honeys" and "my deahs" took over. She did ninety percent of the talking and ninety percent of her subject was K. A. Porter; she was, all the same, really delightful. —I mean by the "all the same" that she showed so little apparent interest in others: I spoke of a mutual friend—Agnes Tait— whom she hasn't seen for years, and she recalled at once their sneaking off from Yaddo to the races—but made no inquiry about Agnes. She did show, though, a serious and attentive excitement in talking of the work of some few of the students; there, she was functioning as older and wiser craftsman. . . . She said she had never thought of being "a success," that always she had tried to be the "best kind of artist" she could be; and that now she has success she can get money for lecturing and has offers from television and Hollywood—but cannot get the kind of money for her actual writing which would insure her time for uninterrupted writing. She told of a year, perhaps in the 1930's, when she was down to $15 and her rent coming due; and suddenly in the mail there arrived a check for $2,500 from the Book of the Month Club—a gift for a writer considered by publishers to be insufficiently rewarded for the quality of her work. "I went right to the bank and deposited it and asked when I could begin to draw on it and they said, 'Why, right away.' And I began to *draw*!" It may have been at this time she wrote *Noon Wine* and *Old Mortality* in fourteen days. I asked if it were true (as I'd heard) that she writes intensely and rapidly or not at all, and she said Yes. She spoke of her novel—which has certainly been rumored for twenty years—and said, "If I could get three uninterrupted months I could finish it." . . . Bob and E. had her talking of some of her stories: "Hacienda"—in which she used Eisenstein and others she saw coldly using the Mexicans. "Rope" —had come "suddenly, like a bubble," after a New York State summer when she'd lived near a variety of young couples, and overheard their quarrels: small quarrels that yet went on and on—"But they never hit too low. The tip was always kept on the sword. And if one said a really dangerous thing, the other deflected it." Bob said he had analyzed "Rope" and found the paragraphs coiling and uncoiling like rope, being knotted and unknotted, snapping every so often with the word "rope." Was he correct? She said the symbol of a theme (which she accidentally spoonerized and was delighted: "the thimble of my—my seam") comes *with* it; she meant, obviously, with little or no consciousness. But Bob appeared pleased; he said, "People beat me over the head because I can't *prove* these things." . . . Both at her lecture and at Bob's house she attacked the Guggenheims and other foundations for the small percentage of creative people whom they help; she said "the guildsman ought to be judged by the guild—but the people who control these things" know nothing about the arts. She thinks "society has receded from the artist" much more than the other way round. "Should the artist cease to speak? No. For some day, some time his words will have value again." What she was regretting though (this is from her platform speech) was the alienation of the artist in modern society: his feeling and society's feeling that he is a special person; his feeling that he is outside (above) the laws of society, and its feeling that he simply does not belong. She wondered if in any other era the artist was not only ignored but often even insulted—and at the least questioned—for what he does. . . . At Bob's she was awfully amusing about her literary honors. She got an honorary degree at a North Carolina college but (Randall Jarrell told her) the board consented to it only on condition that Inglis Fletcher, author of bosomy historical novels and a sister of the Governor of North Carolina, get a doctorate at the same time. And then, back at Stanford where she was teaching, "They still wouldn't give the students credits for my courses because I had no degree." I said: "Look, I have a degree. I'm a Doctor!" But they said, "No." She joshed about "Dr." Edith Sitwell who, KAP says, signs herself both Litt.D. and D.Litt.—"because one is the English and one the American version." . . . "Dr. Porter. Imagine!" . . . All this with much tossing of the head, and laughter. She has pretty feet, is rather a small woman, and was dressed in a cool-looking gray and silver dress: broad, vertical stripes. . . . She had to borrow $450 to fly to New York to get a gold medal from some library crowd. "They put me in a little hotel room for three days. If I stayed longer I'd have to pay my own expenses. And then they gave me a huge dinner at Peer's" (it sounded like; Pierre's?) "and lots of people, and there I was surrounded by laurel—and the medal was handed to me by *Pearl Buck*. And Clifton Fadiman was the master of ceremonies." "Oh, that was all right," said Bob. "Yes, that was all right. After all —that's what he is: a master of ceremonies. So I thought, 'Well, anyway, I can pawn the gold medal.' And I took it to a pawnshop and the man said it was worth $7.50!" . . . She had at last been reading de Sade as, it happened, E. and I had been: and with the same reaction—how dull. "After all, the poor man was shut up in jail for years, and was just dreaming day and night." Some talk of obscenity. She and Bob both thought Lucretius "really lewd." She said as a youngster of thirteen she read Rabelais and others with no consciousness of the dirt, and she feels that if such books were just casually dropped into the lists of youngsters' reading they'd have all their good effects—"opening a whole world"—and leave the kids about as innocent as ever: and that of course such titles would thereby lose their reputation of exciting mystery for adolescents. She decided to leave; we decided to leave; she decided to have one more gin. I said, "Of course it's improper to leave before the Queen—but we have a drive of half an hour or more." That pleased her, Southern belle and all.

I think she specially liked E. . . . As we *were* leaving, I spoke of meeting her again in New Haven, next winter: we're two of this year's Bollingen Poetry Award committee. She wanted to know if I had any book in mind yet; I hadn't; I mentioned that Robert Penn Warren has a narrative poem coming out, which she knew; and there's to be a collected poems by Theodore Roethke. "Who?" "Roethke. R-o-e-t-h-k-e." "Oh, yes. Well, I won't vote for him." I said, "Wallace Stevens won't vote for him. And I won't vote for him." "Good!" she called, sitting at the kitchen table, waving her glass above the carnations. "Good! Let him bring out his old book for all we care!"

●

ONE IS INCLINED to say of most magazine editors that they don't know a good poem from a bad. But yes—yes, they do. How else explain how almost unerringly they keep printing the bad?

●

I NOTICED when Lindsay (thirteen) read aloud a passage from a hunting book the other day he pronounced "genital" as "genteel." I'd love to see a literary history titled "The Genital Tradition."

●

THE OTHER NIGHT in the talk about writers and writing with Katherine Anne Porter, Bob Stallman spoke of the comparatively few grants given to creative writers and of the surprising number of would-be writers working on the Connecticut faculty. I said: Yes, but most of them, given an independent future, would not succeed in writing. This way, they never need prove their lack of talent; this way, they are safely unhappy. . . . Only I did not say that "safely unhappy" phrase, because I didn't think of it till the next day.

•

BOB STALLMAN—whom I saw again the other evening—says he mentioned to Allen Tate his (Stallman's)—(how does one avoid that clumsy construction?)—doing a review for the *Saturday Review*. Tate said Stallman should be ashamed of himself. Stallman then brought up, he says, such names as Dudley Fitts, my own, some others, as occasional *SR* contributors. We should all, said Tate, be ashamed of ourselves. —Meaning, whatever Tate's detailed explanation may have been, that it's a bad magazine. . . . Well, I told Stallman I think in most ways the *SR* is a stupid magazine; but if you write a piece as well and honestly as you can, and the *SR* prints it as is, where's the harm? El's notion was that if you are going to balk at magazines which do things one disapproves of, you are going to be almost out of a market; and she further argued that you might arrogantly consider your contribution to such as the *SR* a step toward better standards. . . . I suppose Tate would argue that any contribution is an assist to undesirable editors. . . . Integrity is a complex problem. Esther Bates recalls a woman who boasted of the many famous men she had slept with, "And oftentimes," the woman said, "during the night I would rise on my elbow and gaze on the sleeping face and think, 'All this within my power!' "

89

LORD DUNSANY in a recent article on Irish writers is cursory on W. B. Yeats and calls AE Ireland's greatest poet. Yeats was too arrogant, too famous, not to be resented by all the little Dunsanys. But how senile to suppose uttering nonsense will make it so. Cf. here, Yeats's poem on the sweating eunuchs as they gaze in hell at Don Juan's naked thigh.

●

PERCEPTION is drunken; execution is sober.

●

I HAVE JUST gone through scrapbooks of the columns, etc., I wrote in high school and college papers. Things I suppose I haven't looked at for twenty to twenty-five years. What overwhelmed me was the sense that the boy and young man wrote as though writing were a way of showing off. . . . I should have come away from the books completely hopeless save that there was some indication of improvement toward the last: an instinctive, slight moving away from self-consciousness.

●

THE HAPHAZARD, unguided ways by which I stumbled around in literature through my boyhood and youth probably necessitate a lifetime trying to purify a critical taste and a reliable way of writing. Will even that much time do?

THE MERETRICIOUS. Katherine Mansfield kept wondering if she were pure in heart.

•

AT THE SIGHT or news of anything of mine in print, my father generally says one of two things: "Will you get money for that?" or "How much will you get for that?" . . . No harm meant. It is the response of a wholly different standard. The standard I grew up with. . . . Ponnie—my great-uncle George Scott—once said to me when I was in college: "Don't decide on a job just because of the money in it. It's better to do something you really want to do." Nobody in my family ever said anything resembling that; nobody in my family—nobody else—would even have conceived of such a remark. . . . Now Ponnie's working record for decades was, as I understand it, one of comparative ease more dependent on his brother's (my grandfather's) initiative than on his own; granted; still, from any of my kin, it was an astounding observation. It was not a remark made in a literary context; I'm sure he was thinking of jobs—not of poetry; but it was certainly intended as a generality, ready for any context.

•

EZRA POUND'S ear is famously praised, and I guess it is often a skillful one; and yet I open to the first of his Cavalcanti sonnets and it begins "You, who do—"

•

THE NAY-SAYING criticism never lasts. It is often of immense value, but in its very nature the value is bound to be temporary.

Think of Mencken. If such criticism is mistaken, it is soon for-gotten. If it is correct, it presumably serves its function; then it is of course forgotten. . . . Well, most criticism—yay or nay—is forgotten; but so is most writing; and the only criticism that sur-vives generations is the positive, creative kind. This is interesting for its consistency with all surviving writing of whatever kind: no great creative art roots in negation.

●

I HAVE a handful of scraps of scribbled notes for this journal and it is time I returned to it and put them in order. I am in Santa Fe, New Mexico, in Jozef Bakos' adobe house at 576 Camino del Monte Sol. We arrived here on September 2nd, intending to stay for a year: to have a startling change from New England. Which it is, and I have been busy with many notes about that—notes not for this journal—and with an acceleration of writing poetry (not, yet, about New Mexico).

●

GOETHE'S REMARK that there was no crime he could not imagine committing sheds no light on his moral character but only on the power of his imagination.

●

I TOLD my wife this was an ancient Chinese proverb, but I had just made it up: The sweetness of the morning depends upon the taste in one's mouth.

I SEE THAT William Carlos Williams remarks in one of his *Selected Essays* that the school of imagism could not last because it had no sense of form. I had not thought of it that way, but this summer I thought of imagism as compared to the methods of, say, Shakespeare, Keats, Whitman—pick whatever great names you choose; and according to the terms of objectivism you can have some good poetry, but never— never— the poetry of the big boys.

●

> One for my master, one for my dame,
> But none for the little boy that cries in
> the lane.

—To what extent is Mother Goose's false rhyming responsible for the general ignorance of what rhyme is?

●

PERHAPS IT IS time to write an article In Defense of Blank Verse. Most attempts to avoid it in writing "natural-sounding" verse are no better than avoidance: a negative way, they turn out to sound more artificial. No, the variation of blank verse is, I suspect, infinite; everything depends on the power of the poet. Any generation will give you many Stephen Phillipses, only one Robinson.

●

WHAT A BOON to the world if someone were able to set down the data under the heading: How to Tell Minor Poetry When You Write It.

I DAYDREAM that a member of an audience says to me afterward, "What kind of poet would you call yourself, Mr. Scott?" "Persistent."

•

SOME POETS, far from old, seem to dry up and disappear completely. What's become of Sidney Salt? of Clark Mills? Why—another question—are the pretty boys never really any good? Gilbert Maxwell, Lionel Wiggam, George Dillon. That forsythia talent, again; and I suspect that in some instances it is an extension of youthful male beauty. Frederic Prokosch almost scrambled through, but I'm afraid not really.

•

HOW FAR this New Mexican land is from Concord, Massachusetts, yet the first week I was here I sat on the floor at a party while artists Karl Larsson and Philip McClosson exchanged Emerson and Thoreau quotations. Those Concord men get around. Larsson came to the U.S. as a youth from Sweden—knew for awhile only two English words, "born" and "died," which he learned cutting gravestones in Vermont. A school teacher there got him to reading Emerson.

•

LIVING IN the neighborhood I have taken to reading the books on Lawrence by those (incredibly) still surviving women up in Taos. Frieda has the last word, always: for one thing, after all, she had Lawrence, and nobody got him away from her either; for another, there's no nonsense about her; for another, though she's an amateur, at her best she can write better than the others—see the moving restraint of the death chapter at the end of *Not I, but the Wind*. . . . Mabel Luhan's imperceptiveness is revealed when she is pursuing her theory that Lawrence was too much in Frieda's grasp. Now Frieda herself has boasted that Lawrence took a lot of his ideas from her, and perhaps he did; but the Luhan's contention of course is that Lawrence was being strangled (by, I should say, the wrong woman). And Luhan tells of an occasion when they all got out to wonder at a magnificent view—somewhere around here. Lawrence said nothing. Frieda broke into an ecstasy of admiration. Then presently Lawrence began to comment. There, Mabel Luhan thinks, is an illustration of Lawrence's pitiful dependence upon his wife. I don't think so at all. I think it very *like* a creative, sensitive person not to babble o' green fields the moment he looks upon them; it's precisely the noncraftsman who rushes in, in daily occurrences such as these, while your artist preserves his secret, spying silence. He knows by instinct and training that there is too much or too little to be said for him to jump into what must, offhand, be the supererogation of talk. He plots his responses, he manages his recording; and this is not done by hasty commonplaces in the style of a postcard to the folks back home. This, I am certain, is what was going on with Lawrence, and this is the last process Mabel Luhan would comprehend. She is no artist; she is one of those bystanders who confuse art with their own emotions.

•

ARTHUR MILLER's *Crucible*, his play about the Salem witches: why is it unsuccessful? Because he wrote the significance of it, not the play. It is therefore the representation of a thing, not the thing itself. It is a pageant, not a play.

95

DICK EBERHART told me a little story about Phelps Putnam. Robert Lowell gave a reading at Harvard and—whatever the year was—Lowell was then the new white-headed boy in American poetry. Into the front row swept Putnam in wide black hat, and cloak, looking like a Cantabridgean ghost of Baudelaire: Putnam, almost famous for having written and published nothing in all the years after his first two books. Almost famous—almost forgotten: such lines met in him. He just drank. Well, after the reading he was cordially annexed by Lowell, Eberhart, one or two others: they sat around a nearby restaurant; and soon, politely, Putnam was asked if he'd been doing any writing. He had. From his pocket he took, Dick tells me, "a thin sheaf of obscene poems." About a week later his death was in the papers.

●

FROM THE RECENT lyrics I have seen, I judge Archibald MacLeish is now in a late-Yeats phase. It won't wash, as Mark Twain would say. What a strange career! You can't take away from him the honor of having done some beautiful things—the "Marvell," some passages in "Conquistador"; but the Pound-Eliot indebtedness was basic for years; now this. I was told years ago Eliot wondered who "the real MacLeish" might be behind it all. Of course, MacLeish worked up his borrowings far more skillfully than did his contemporary John Peale Bishop, yet he remains in that devastating category of Picasso's—those who come after the innovators and "make it pretty." . . . Probably Edmund Wilson's parody of MacL. says it all; that cruelest of parodies.

THE KIND of sweet, apologetic look of the middle-aged critic who started life as a poet.

•

THE ONE sane wish a writer can make: to write something better than he has ever written before.

•

DESIRE CANNOT make poems; only a driving necessity can: necessity is stronger than desire. . . . I thought this last May and out of it I made an X-diagram of shuttling arrows: N and S—mind and body, imagination and desire; E and W, consciousness and a real thing, significance and the fact. Where the two shuttling lines cross, center, there is the necessity which accomplishes art. . . . The other day I made at least a sort of poem of this. Verses anyway.

•

I'M NOT interested in making pretty sounds—I try to make sounds.

•

THOMAS REED POWELL, professor emeritus of law at Harvard, was at the Hampton house one evening last winter. He is an old friend of Robert Frost. He told me: "I said to Frost, 'You're a pretty good poet, Robert. But when these young men come and sit around your feet, you talk politics to them. Why do you do that?' And Frost said, 'I do it so they won't ask me questions about poetry.' "

●

POETRY CANNOT be achieved by an act of will; but there are ways of living, involving the will, which will help or hinder the writing of poetry.

●

ARTIST AND CHILD: the things everybody says—we all say—about the childlikeness (or, if you please, childishness) of the artist. The charge, to a point, is true; and I have been thinking there is an explanation not at all unflattering to the artist. Everything that happens to a child is important: this is the merit of his "self-centeredness." The artist more or less preserves this ability into his adult life. Indeed his greatest fear should be to lose it. His next greatest, not to control it. . . . The inferior artist, of course, is a confused being: he *really* gets a sensation of self-importance blocking his view of the *thing*—he makes a fatal transferral, as though an adding machine assumed mathematics nonexistent outside the machine itself. Then, very likely, this type of artist tries—as Jack Wheelwright said of Harry Crosby—to live his art, not to live *for* his art; which, as I recall Jack added, is difficult enough.

I HAVE MADE no entries in this journal since October 1954 though I have now and then scribbled notes for use in it. I sit here wondering how to account for a year and a half? I have written some poems—and have sent out a new collection as *Scrimshaw*. I have spent much time on prose—written a new essay or two and revised and arranged and sent out a book of them as *Free to Stay*. My adhesive long poem, *The Dark Sister*, has been out but now languishes on the shelf: publication seems hopeless. I wrote 20 or 25,000 words of a book designed to a rambling pattern of the year in which we traveled from Connecticut to New Mexico, but I felt discouraged over it and let it go in frustration: I thought if most of my prose and—in book form—my poetry is considered "fine but unsalable," nobody will want this sort of book. A mean reason for not writing something, but a potent one. I also play with a notion of writing something about John Sloan in the Southwest and have collected materials but do not as yet see the best way to handle it.

During all these months I have now and then met or visited or entertained some literary people: J. B. Priestley and Jacquetta Hawkes; William Carlos Williams and his wife; Selden Rodman and his; Paul Horgan; Robinson Jeffers. I may later put down some things about them in this notebook. And of course have seen much of the local lights—Oliver LaFarge, Witter Bynner, Haniel Long.

The rest of the account is non-literary—illness, travel, and, finally, buying a house and having our things moved here. We are now at 550 East Alameda, in Santa Fe: a "permanent" address.

•

I SHALL BEGIN the gathering up of notes and scraps for the journal with some comments I set down, during the week I was in

99

hospital, about the newly published volume of Yeats's letters.

I find interesting the mental lechery of Yeats's last years. First, there are the tender letters to Olivia Shakespeare, who had once been his mistress. But these seem to stop when he has new, young women to whom he likes to write intimate things. Especially curious is the boy-girl, girl-boy mixup declared in one of his letters to Dorothy Wellesley. Why this dependence on women? It is perhaps only the conventional old goat wearing—after all— an embroidered coat. The pinching, stroking old man happens to be the poet and theorist Yeats. He says that poets would be lost without women—poets even choose their men friends from those with whom they can talk of women. Questionable: this huge self-projection upon women exclusively.

An island. To combat that island's ignorance is Yeats's great literary passion. Does he then root from that ignorance? Yeats's obliviousness to so much outside is a remarkable limitation. Nothing touched him deeply except Irishry. This was perhaps necessary to his art—enforced his frame of reference. But the *confidence* accompanying all this! His judgments—when made —of American and even English figures are usually ridiculous. And within Ireland their "greatest" are assumed to be "the greatest" in the world. Again, was this necessary to him? Perhaps; but how narrowingly provincial at the same time. . . . For example, he writes of Paul Manship as the greatest American sculptor, of Luytens as the greatest living architect. He simply didn't know what he was talking about. If he glances at any American poetry, it is Elinor Wylie and Edna Millay he notices: the *feminine tradition* with no peculiarly American tone. . . . I mean by all this: it is healthy for us to recognize Yeats's limitations. I think they can be traced down and co-ordinated through small particulars. Then let him stay, as he is, a great poet, but no longer overwhelming us.

Note: his repeated insistence upon *Personality*.

It is amusing, examining his ego, that in his letters he wonders if the great poetic age is over? That is, of course, he wonders about this late in his own life. And didn't he in a public speech advise young Irish writers to turn to realistic prose? He did.

As yet we have no published letters to Maud Gonne; but the tone of his letters to Olivia Shakespeare makes me more than ever suspect that Maud Gonne was—as I have theorized somewhere in this journal—a myth in his life, a useful symbol for his poetry. Note his emotional immaturity: his hectic attempts at marriage. Iseult Gonne says No, so off he hies himself within the week to George. Then, later years, his marriage established and his children born, he indulges in lecherous relationships— by letter, anyway—with younger women. (Actual bedding?) He is an exhibitionist in words.

●

ROBERT GRAVES is currently attacking the work of Yeats, Eliot, Pound, Auden, and Dylan Thomas. As yet I have seen only a small portion of what Graves has written. But this could be the beginning of the end of their reign, coming from Graves. Attacks by an old fuddyduddy such as Alfred Noyes or attacks out of the exacerbated disappointments of Robert Hillyer are futile. But Graves just now has been critically elevated to a top notch among contemporary poets and so he speaks from a potent position, above suspicion of any meretricious reason.

●

THE OLD QUESTION, again, of what is sentimental. I have been remembering a newspaper story of a few years back about the death of a little boy. The boy's father in a fit of temper beat the child fatally. Before the boy died at the hospital he said, "I still love you, Daddy." Now that really happened. Children being children, it is beyond all doubt credible. But could it be used in writing without seeming a blatant bid for tears? I know no answer except, also, the old one: everything depends on *how* it is done.

●

Literary History

When Robinson was young
Who cared that he sung?
While every critical prick
Was raised to George Sylvester Viereck.

Perhaps I should annotate that. I recently read that in the early 1900's the New York Times Sunday Book Review devoted two successive front pages to admiring discussion of Viereck's poetry. In some ways the world *don't* move. I would say to any young critic, have all the theories you want but don't neglect literary history.

●

MY FRIEND Al Rosenfeld, who works the Southwest for the Luce empire, says wistfully: "I don't have time for *unnecessary* writing."

RECENTLY I RECALLED something that touches me deeply. It happened long ago, probably within the year after my first book was published. I met a young painter in Providence—Florence Leif, who was and still is a very good painter—and she told me she could not afford to buy my book and so she borrowed a copy and had made a complete typescript of it. One such gesture may not quiet me, or anybody, for a lifetime, but perhaps it should.

•

THAT WEEK I was hospitalized I read, also, a great deal in Matthiessen's anthology of American poetry. When I encountered a poem especially exciting to me my spine did not (as heretofore) prickle, but my operated-upon left knee. (The operation by the way had been performed under spinal injection, which may be a relevant detail.) Anyway, the second week I noted prickle still in the knee but beginning to quaver in the spine. Yet the fifth week the knee sensation still occurred. . . . A month or so ago I got a line out of this: "where the wound is, one responds."

•

KEN LASH's prayer: "Oh, God! Just lemme have an open drawer where I can t'row me pomes!"

•

WHY WHEN I have a prose thing published do I usually read it over and over but when the published poem arrives I often delay looking at it and often only glance hurriedly through it? When this question first occurred to me I had no answer. Now I think the answer is: fear of disappointment in the more important thing, the poem: fear I shall lose the conviction or illusion that it is a good poem. Not that I can't always—always—find something in the prose to improve upon; but it matters less.

•

LOOKING OUT at the Jemez Mountains and listening to Berlioz on the record player, I thought, amidst the phrasing of the end of the Second Movement in *Harold in Italy*, what is the Romantic Movement except this—the excess, the "unnecessary," the unexpected overflow? And why not? Who between Pope and Keats will not, if choice must be made, choose Keats? As the horribly clever Auden has observed, the Romantic Movement will return. And why not? It is individualist tradition, the Protestant Tradition. In some such manner only can we be saved.

•

AS TO MERRILL MOORE's poetry: at least one can say the fraudulence is innocent. . . . I suppose one can say that of lots of people's poetry.

•

D. H. LAWRENCE's poetry: it is not quite good enough. Unlike Hardy's, the clumsiness of the poems strikes one not as deliberate but as helpless, hurried, amateurish. (Probably too much of all Lawrence's writing must be so characterized. In his forty-odd years he turned out an impressive amount, but how good—really—is most of it?) . . . Graves by the way has the Hardy touch. Whether indebted or not I don't know, and it's no matter since Graves has his own way of going at things. It is his unexpected subject and his complexly-plain way of dealing with it that are remindful of Hardy. So that you are moved both in the mind and in the nerves.

●

LAST SUNDAY saw the U.S. premiere of Sir Lawrence Olivier's film, *Richard III*. (More audience in that single three-four broadcast than in the total of all the many stage performances since Shakespeare wrote the play; so we were told.) One commentator wonders if now *Richard III* will draw as a film in the movie houses or if TV "killed it at one stroke?" I will bet against the killing. (It was a box-office failure.) You don't say of a good poem, "I've read it so I won't read it again." Not at all. *Because* it is a good poem and you have read it you will go on reading it. . . . Of no other kinds of writing is this reaction necessarily true.

●

PREFACES TO BOOKS: they can be as impertinent as an explanatory card pinned up beside a painting. To be good they must function. . . . Foster Damon used to say: put in your Preface what you want the critics and reviewers to say. I think he got that tactical notion from Amy Lowell.

KATHERINE MANSFIELD's worry that she was not "pure enough" to write greatly? —Could one by some kind of thought, some kind of intellectual fasting, attain purity as a writer? To forget all but the art itself—practise it day in and out happily: without thought of others or of extraneous things, or anything but the art itself?

•

THE 1955 Bollingen Prize went to Louise Bogan and Léonie Adams. Thus bypassed were a new book by Jeffers and the *Collected Poems* of Cummings. It is that Wallace Stevens (who very likely called the tune in committee meeting: he always did at any committee meeting where I observed him) was put off by the strength of the bigger talents? I know Stevens did not like Jeffers' work or Cummings' either; no doubt honestly. But what to him were the fragile talents of Bogan and Adams? Well, there's no challenge or offense in them. . . . Stevens has died since I last made any of these notes. An honorable man. But I incline to agree with Rodman (who visited us last week) that the talent is essentially decorative and is at present greatly overestimated.

•

I HAVE FOUND in Gissing's *Ryecroft* a summary for our overweaningly critical era: "Principles always become a matter of vehement discussion when practice is at ebb."

•

ONE MIGHT, rounding a corner and coming unexpectedly upon

a friend, say the three words he would always remember; or rounding the corner of a thousand pages, write the two lines that will last.

•

WHAT A RELAXATION it must be to say, as Eliot has, "I, as a minor poet . . ."

•

ON HIS DEATHBED that charming man Ridgely Torrence lamented to his wife that he had not worked harder and accomplished more. He once—to me—gently struck his chest and said, "I have all the machinery in here that Frost has but I lack the dynamo."

•

PROBABLY THE THING about Yeats is simply this: when he wrote out of his extraordinary sensibilities he wrote greatly; when he operated merely from cerebration he often uttered nonsense. Years ago, I remember, in reviewing a bunch of books having to do with him, I used as my text that remark of Santayana's: "I am an ignorant man—almost a poet."

•

EVERY WRITER should know Kipling's profound observation:

that perhaps Shakespeare got the drowning of Ophelia from once having seen a kitten drowned.

•

IT SEEMS to me the older I get the more rapidly I must talk. Otherwise the more chance of being interrupted. I should like trying to think things slowly and to say them slowly and to be replied to the same way. That could all be so peaceful and so exciting, so restful and so enriching. But now nobody conducts himself in such a way or would succeed if he tried. *I* aim to be a good listener and usually I am a good listener, though often I am bored. But this adherence of mine is not pure: I like to be liked and will suffer fools and much else in the cause. No, it is as though we are all dislodged stones in the stream now—tumbled along. Mostly the best talk I know is shrill with liquor: talk, that is, at its frankest, most uninhibited, excited, and far-ranging. Not the same qualities, though, as consideration and wisdom. . . . The natural acceleration of older years in life must indeed be aggravated in our era. All this has to do, of course, with our writing.

•

FOR EXAMPLE, Robert Penn Warren's novels: open them to any page and could you say, "This is Warren"? No. The prose is anonymous. Ultimately what other test of a writer is there except personality? No matter what a writer writes about—from whatever moral, religious, sociological, philosophical view—what in art matters? Tone. Style. The individual, unmistakable voice. The *way* the thing is said.

108

OFF AND ON since last May I have been writing a book about my Newport childhood—to be called *The Owl in the Hall* and to be published God knows when. By mid-August or so I had about 20,000 words down; four chapters. For the past two months I have done nothing on it either, because I wasn't well or because I was busy with other stuff. This morning, as I had planned yesterday, I returned to it—reading over the manuscript so far to get warmed up to write more. . . . Now: last night I dreamed that I stood—it seemed for just a moment—with various relatives of mine, all dead. Nearest me was my Grandfather Scott. At first he stood side-to and I noted the generous sweep of his mustache. Then he turned and I stood very near him and he looked kindly toward me and I looked right at him. I never saw him more clearly or more accurately in life (he has been dead eighteen years) than I saw him last night. He was dressed in trousers and a sleeveless undershirt, the way he would be of a Sunday morning when he sloshed around the garage washing the car; and I noticed the freckled skin of his arms and shoulders— *which in consciousness I had not recalled.* That is my first point here. The second is: I thought, I am dreaming and isn't this wonderful for my book that I can bring him back this way and see him exactly as he was. (And a part of my thought was an implication, or supposition, that perhaps I could continue to do this in other dreams of other dead relatives and friends.) . . . I did not, however, recall the dream until I was reading my manuscript this morning. This noon I told El of it. She said Erich Fromm once told her that almost always consciousness of dreaming while dreaming is confined to the "creative" or "artistic" types: a psychoanalyst does not customarily find it in other types. . . . And as Fromm has said in one of his books (Have I quoted this before? I am always quoting it), "There is no 'as if' in the dream." You are "really" there: the other person is "really" there. That seemed spectacularly so as I faced my Grandfather Scott. . . . I think that was all the dream. That nothing was said. I think as the little dream began I saw and knew perfectly well who the others in the group were; but I cannot recapture that. . . . If only I were mystic-minded, I could interpret his benign gaze upon me as an O.K. from another world upon the truth I have told about him in my book. But alas I am not mystic; nor even Irish.

•

BEWARE OF ALL poems that have news value.

•

AGAIN, THE interruption to this journal—this letter to myself—has been a long one. As no doubt I have recorded before, such interruptions are—to me—a good sign: I am generally busy with more creative work. The Newport childhood book, *The Owl in the Hall*, was completed late in February: that is to say, 65,000 words are on paper and the manuscript is in a box in a drawer. In time I shall tinker with it; I already have a thing or two in mind to add to it; and I have preserved my unhurried attitude toward it. As I damn well have to. There are just enough family skeletons in it to make me feel it cannot be published in the near future. Not that it is a scandalous book; such passages are very small and very few, and yet my conviction is that they are necessary to the story. And I am not sitting here impatient for anybody's death, I may add. . . . Esther Bates, who visited us in March for a couple of weeks, is the only person so far to read the manuscript and she was approving.

The months on *The Owl*—from May, 1956 to this February—gave me next to no verse, of course. I was obsessed and absorbed by the Newport years and content to take a vacation from poetry. Now I am itchy to make poems again, and I have done a few. One of them, "Come Green Again," may be good but of course I am not sure.

During the Newport stretch I took time out for a long essay on my first year in the Southwest, almost 10,000 words. I thought it an unsalable monster, but no; with—I trust—slight cutting it will appear this fall. And meanwhile other essays and poems have been appearing and so, along with the book reviewing stints I persist in doing, I have been "'all over the place" despite the fact that so much of these very months have been spent in writing for that box in that drawer.

Since I last wrote in this journal, *The Dark Sister* has been taken and will be published this coming fall. The process of this little miracle is probably worth recording as an example of the vagaries of publishing poetry.

First, to recapitulate: my old publisher, Macmillan, would not take it. Perhaps four or five others in New York followed a pattern; there were one or two that sent the manuscript swiftly back, but several hugged it for months—six and eight months—and then gave me the congratulatory letter of rejection: it was, they said, a beautiful work and they so much hoped that somebody (else) would publish it. In some desperation I tried the small press Alan Swallow runs in Denver, and from him I heard that *The Dark Sister* was a very good story but "not poetry." After that the manuscript stayed here on the shelf, unopened, as returned from Swallow. (Not that I believed Swallow's dictum, but I was at a loss.)

Now to begin at the new beginning: a year or more ago M. L. Rosenthal sent me a copy of *The Nation*, of which he is poetry editor, with an article on contemporary poetry. I acknowledged it. He replied, I think asking to see poems, and soon he did publish one or two of mine, and then last summer he came to the University of New Mexico as a visiting lecturer from New York University and we met and became friends.

To go on. (This reminiscing is tiresome.)

He arranged a lecture and reading for me at the University and among other things I read a passage from *The Dark Sister*. Mack asked to see the manuscript, returned it from New York under the impression that another copy of it was being held by some publisher. We got this straightened out and the manuscript went to the New York University Press.

Presently Mack telephoned to say the Press editors were enthusiastic but, before they faced the business interests could I fetch some encomiums. I did—and this is the best reason, if there are any reasons, to record these adventures: the instant kind response I got from Horace Gregory (as ever), Malcolm Cowley, Lee Anderson, Richard Eberhart, and Dr. Williams. They poured their letters in at once.

So it went. From Wilson Follett, head editor at the Press, I received a carbon of his report: the kind of once-in-a-lifetime report which should obviate all a writer's wretched days.

Now the Press has delayed the book until January, '58; I don't know why. I have, since last April, read galley and pageproofs; retrieved *Free to Stay*, my book of essays, and *Scrimshaw*, my book of poems, revised both and sent them on to the Press where they now repose.

•

ANNE PARRISH died on September 5th. And E. and I failed to get to see her when we were back east last June. My regrets are lifelong. So far as I know, the papers have paid scant attention to her death; it is long since *The Perennial Bachelor* and *All Kneeling*, the years of her first fame; and yet some of her later novels were better—*Pray for a Tomorrow* is a remarkable allegory, *Poor Child* an unforgettable drama of the pathos of love; I think she was our best current woman novelist. But toward the last she was ignored and half-forgotten.

Some years ago I published an admiring essay on her novels. It pleased her. It was not well written (as no doubt she knew: she was an excellent craftsman). It was not well written because months had elapsed between my reading and making notes and my writing; then I think I was not wholly convinced of some of the things I said—friendship, affectionate regard, can tie one up so; finally, I felt intimations of deeper biographical sources in her novels than it seemed possible to explore. My suspicion is that within Anne Parrish there existed the catty, selfish, security-seeking, vain woman whom she excoriated in so many novels. She herself made an advantageous marriage—she, the daughter of impecunious painter parents—with a rich man (Charles Corliss) much older than herself. Because of this she lived—I knew her in her last decade—in a splendid house between her pond and her woods, her gardens, the interior rich with Renoirs, and so on; but, then, lonely and never ceasing to mourn Josiah Titzell, the young husband who had lived but a few years: his room kept as it was, zebra-decorated glasses, a merry-go-round zebra and whatnot zebras everywhere because Jo had loved zebras; his ashes buried outside her wnidow. I feel sure that her illnesses of the last years were basically psychosomatic: her partial blindness not least.

Yet she stayed beautiful even in her late sixties. She was small, fragile—in a lovely way girlish. A worn but still beautiful Dresden. She all but lived in isolation with her longtime chauffeur

Maurice and her cook Lucy. She was an unexpectant princess locked and old in a castle. Whenever I was at her house I got feeling bullishly awkward, as though I might at any moment displease a lady easily displeased.

And yet—it is so hard to phrase these various views accurately —I was very fond of her (and of course, to begin with, I admired her work), and I've reason to believe she was genuinely fond of E. and myself. We wrote each other with some frequency—I have many letters—and last winter she sent us a hooked rug she had made for us.

I am sure she was hurt by the neglect of her work in the latter (and, really, more serious, most mature) years. She told me she had been informed that Katherine Anne Porter and Glenway Wescott had laughed at the suggestion she be elected (amongst them!) to the National Academy of Arts or whatever it's called. (She wrote me some wonderfully catty letters about Porter— "the Living Legend.") She was pleased a few months ago when I wrote her that I. J. Kapstein had told me he kept some of her novels on his students' reading list at Brown.

She was at work, very slowly, on a new novel; of course I have no idea how far into it she had gone.

I have many memories of her even though I saw her only a few times. I think sometime I shall re-do what I have had to say about her novels and very likely write *her* into it at the same time.

—I was about to leave her, but I find myself sitting here and remembering matters inappropriately conceited to anything I might write for publication about her. One night at dinner at Quantness—her house—(Margaret Emerson Bailey was there) —she said, "My novels are all about love, but nobody knows that except Win." . . . Once she told me that when she first read a poem of mine called "'Day of the Russets" she had tossed the book down on her bed "and bawled." . . . One day when E. and I were there for lunch—Mary Powers to whom *All Kneeling* is dedicated was there—it was a time when Anne's eyesight was bad—and I read her the poems, "Memento," in memory of my mother. From the line "The wind in the rockingchair" on, I could feel Anne's terrific tension; so it seemed. When I got done she was crying. She said nothing, but strode to the fireplace and tossed some Kleenex in; still said nothing. So I said, "Is it all right, Anne?" "NO," she said, "of course it isn't *'all right'*! The things you can do to people!" . . . She was tremendously pleased by my review of her last novel, *And Have Not Love*. I asked to review it for the *Herald-Tribune* and I wanted to, yet it was a difficult job just because I had read galley and page-proofs for her—had even altered a little (somebody had to) a couple of obviously mixed-up sentences. "The review of my lifetime," she wrote me. And I set that down not in conceit but because I am happy to have made her happy. She deserved good words for her novels and I think, after the great success of her earlier work, she got little intelligent or perceptive attention. —I recall a headline over a review of *Poor Child*, in effect "a novel in pastels." Good God! The color is blood.

She was an artist who, by her first marriage, was enabled to live like a great lady—indeed she was that too. I suspect, as I said to begin with, a dichotomy in her life because of all this. And I don't think she gave up either one; certainly she went on refining her art all her life; within herself, though, she may have felt a compromised, not altogether honest, position—perhaps that she had married into the very world of endowed complacency toward which her tongue could be sharpest. That she had as a human being sold out but was determined as an artist not to sell out. . . . But then, too, there is the Titzell romance and what that did to her life. All this, impudent speculation on my part perhaps; but serious; the impudency modulated, at least, by her death.

She once had a baby—born dead, or it was born defective and quickly died. I remember she said, "I never saw it." When? By whom?

I don't know what she felt about Corliss. Margaret Emerson Bailey remembered seeing Anne in her young heyday and with Corliss, and that Corliss seemed "a very old man" beside Anne. Aside from Jo Titzell, her deep attachment was to her brother Dillwyn. Jo's and his deaths occurred, I think, within a year. And Anne's dominating mother (here again, this has to be weighed) lived on to about the same time. She was the model for the terrible, selfish Clara in *And Have Not Love*.

Another thing, an important thing, about Ann Parrish. I have mentioned her beauty, her smallness, her fragility. Yes. But one felt, also, a ramrod in that back. Loss, grief, error, illness, whatever beset her—one felt, even, she would rather be dead than alive without Jo—yet, yet she went on writing. Her excuse for being? No doubt. But the drive was very strong. The great talent was wholly genuine. Even in her last years you could not quite say her loveliness looked "brittle," for there was that strength, a sense almost of an underlying "hardness."

For a brief while just after the first time I had been at Quantness she was annoyed with me. (This probably seeded my bull-in-the-china-shop notion of the following years.) In the midst of some indiscreet remarks of hers—we had had lots of martinis—I said, "Go ahead: I'm a newspaperman but I won't print anything about this." I meant, of course, *this*. She assumed I meant to say nothing in print about her personally. So I discovered a week or two later after I had published a column—perfectly discreet—about visiting her. There was a silence I felt was ominous; then, at last, a letter saying she saw no point in sulking in a mist, that she had been annoyed—but then, perhaps, a little curious and pleased, etc. She was sweet about it and I think eventually forgot all about it.

Last winter here in Santa Fe I met neighbors of hers, literary agents who lived on Peaceable Street. They did not know her. They felt she was a recluse and intimated that the town felt she was cold and aloof. They said that on the day World War II ended they happened to drive by Quantness and saw Anne, Miss Lucy, and Maurice marching round the garden, a little procession of three, waving American flags.

I think she had the hard insensitivity that flashes every now and then with peculiar coldness in people of exceptional sensitivity.

She wore beautiful dresses. She had a little conservatory where she tended all sorts of plants. Her house was jammed with books in no order or arrangement at all. She owned a chair that had belonged to Dr. Johnson. The most, and most beautiful, autumn crocuses I ever saw were all across the lawn between her front windows and the pond. The last time E. and I were there she showed us dwarf iris she was trying to raise. I have since seen the plant here in the Southwest. This part of the country meant much to her because of its association with Jo, I suppose. And she was born in Colorado.

•

ABOUT A YEAR AGO I read a novel of Paul Horgan's called *The Common Heart*, published some fifteen years back. When I next ran into Paul I asked him if he were the little Irish boy with the widowed mother. No, but he "had known a boy like that."

All right, I said: then, what about the lady novelist? Is that Anne Parrish?

Paul's face went bright red. "How did you get that?"

"Well," I said, "I know Anne and I was reminded of her."

"Nobody," Paul said, "has ever spotted that. Keep my secret, will you?"

He and I talked of her death when I saw him a few days ago. "A charming person," he said; "and so much talent!" Yes; and yet, as I surmised to begin with here, her death was barely noticed in the public prints. And I recall that a few years ago when I finished my essay on her novels I first tried *The Saturday Review* and got a rejection note from Amy Loveman saying the magazine preferred to carry a special article on "contemporary writers only"! . . . Weeks after her obituaries, much longer stories hit the papers about her having left ten million dollars.

•

AMONG THE REASONS for reading criticism, one of them is never admitted: that it is easier to read than the thing itself. It asks less of one.

•

INCOMPLETION IS the teaser. Is art attracted by what is incomplete? All life, in a sense? But we can see it best—feel it best—in the specific episode.

•

THORNTON WILDER says "the grand style" is impossible in our time. Probably it will come again. Anyway, he adds, "I no longer think comedy is just a second prize." (This in conversation: Wilder was here for a week recently.)

●

AFTER SO LONG an interval I mean to put into clear typing, and in some instances to put into prose at the same time, the odds and ends I have scribbled down in the pages of my manuscript book.

●

IS THE JEFFERS concept of mankind notably different from Mark Twain's? No. It amounts to the same thing, without humor. Both see life as a trap, as essentially beautiful but insignificant, as ultimately hopeless. And I might add, the views of both are summed up in Housman's poem "Be still, my soul, be still, the arms you bear are brittle . . ."

●

IN THE ACADEMIC world we are often asked to regard as high standards of criticism what are in fact the mean-minded, un-imaginative, envious attitudes of castrati.

●

ONE TIME and another, I have written several poems having to do with kite-flying. They are, perhaps, among my more successful poems. But in "real" life I am and always have been among the clumsiest failures at kite-flying. . . . Not "but" there, but "and"?

•

WE DON'T WANT for art the dramatic moment—we want in art the ordinary moment made dramatic.

•

BEWARE OF BECOMING the kind of person who likes to have his friends (or contemporaries) fail.

•

ALMOST ALL literary criticism is dead when written and buried when published.

•

CAN YOU REFORM your mind in mid-life? Can you in some sense sweep out much of your literary preoccupations and loyalties— replace them—outgrow them—improve them? (So much of what stays in my mind dates from my youthful reading. So much of the world's great literature is still unknown to me.) Or have you by that time of life pretty much fastened upon the things meaningful to you and they won't essentially change?

IF ONE CAN'T write poetry, one can always write a long poem. (This is not really true.)

•

HOLD FAST to what you have come to believe. For instance, don't be thrown by some critic's casual dismissal of Whitman—or Robinson—or whomever. Trust that your long-held conviction of such excellence *must* have a reasonable basis. Trust, even, that you may be the *more* perceptive, sensitive, intelligent reader. . . . To do this is important for many reasons, but not least for your own steadiness of mind, your wholeness, and thereby your own work.

•

THORNTON WILDER praised my "tactful" use of alliteration. A delicious choice of word—tactful.

•

HERE IS a useful analogy. If you contrast amateur acting and the successful, real thing, you can see in the amateur the essence— it is showing-off. The difference in achieved (or great) acting is a showing forth. The individual creates something beyond himself, more than himself, bigger than himself. That self, unlike the amateur's, is not displayed—it is used. —These may be useful terms to apply to poetry or any of the arts.

REPEATEDLY I HAVE dreams involving travel. But not really travel. Rather the dreams are of frustration (and fear), for almost always they are about my trying to get to the train—to the ship—time running out and all sorts of hindrances to my getting there. I never do get there.

•

BEN BAGDIKIAN says that Dick Eberhart told him that I think through prose to poetry. This I take it was intended as description, not as denigration. Is it true? Ben thought not. At the least it represents Dick's apprehension of a poetry very different from his own. . . . Later: Dick is correct.

•

A POEM IS perceived emotionally and is more or less involved with the intellect. Or it is an intellectual perception expressed in more or less emotional language. (Can I have this both ways?)

•

DISTORTION MAY be, it occurs to me, another way of expressing that "stain of personality" which I so harp upon as the indispensable mark of the true poet. In distinctive art (we see it more readily in painting but it goes for poetry and all the rest) it is the distortion—however slight—which proves the master. It *is* the style.

IN MUSIC if you want birdsong don't introduce notes literally imitating birdsong: suggest it, approximate it, use it. (Apply this to writing.)

•

TO GO BACK to Fromm's "as if"—"There is no 'as if' in the dream": the people are *there*, etc. I dreamed of being in a taxi, in the rain, with a girl. (And there was more of it.) How actual, how real, it all was. But, this is a girl whom I know. The reality, then, was all for me. *She* had no experience of it. Therefore the reality of the dream is not to be equated with the reality of experience. At best, the dream halves such reality. Can it be said, then, that it takes two to make reality? As it takes two to create life, two ideas—images—crossing to start a poem? Was Thoreau real at Walden Pond, or Beston in his Outermost House, until each crossed himself with writing a book?

•

THOSE PASSAGES in romantic music where the various themes are upgathered, like so many brooks, into a massive river—and let flood in one great commingling into a sea of sound.

•

SO MANY POETS are damned with faint plays.

ALAS, I SUPPOSE the difference between *Tom Sawyer* and *The Owl in the Hall* is the difference between Tom and his brother Sid.

•

NO HURRY about reviewing poetry. And that's correct—there's no hurry about poetry.

•

WE WENT to hear Emlyn Williams do *A Boy Grows Up*—the Dylan Thomas prose. It was often amusing and charming, yet not altogether satisfactory. There was too much overdoing in the material itself—too much farce and meaningless bravura. Eloquence and lyric splendor, both present, were overshadowed by rhetoric. A revelation of putting on the paint thick instead of achieving depth. No, this is Thomas' left hand. When Williams concluded with "And Death Shall Have No Dominion," we were taken up to a wholly different level: there were true power and significance.

•

IT OCCURS to me that Emily Dickinson's collected poems constitute one of the chapters in America's great town tradition. (Not to limit them only to that.) They come so integrally out of the streets, weathers, gardens, seasons, people, and deaths of a particular community that they form—at least in a transcendental way—a forerunner to Tilbury Town, Spoon River, Winesburg, and Grover's Corners.

ARE PUNS FUN because they are a kind of rhyme? From Shake-speare to Auden, an awful lot of poets delight in puns. It's not, I think, poets who assume the customary look of anguish when a pun is made.

•

A POEM SHOULD evolve from its inner necessity to its outer form. It is like architecture.

•

BIOGRAPHY IS a sieve-through. It has to be. It cannot be any-thing else but a choice residue, all the minutiae of daily living lost while the "significant" things remain—the things usually obscured in the actual living. . . . Yet I would rather read biog-raphy, I sometimes think, than anything else.

•

ISN'T OSCAR WILDE one of the expendable literary gents? What other writer so minor lingers on decade after decade with so much reputation? For what did he accomplish beyond a couple of bright plays? The fictions are slight. The poems are simply damned poor. It must, then, be his legend—the legend of a bril-liant talker and an arrogantly eccentric man. Yet there have been other such, dimly recalled as incidents in biographies and mem-oirs of important people. It may, more, be the still continuing excitement of his scandalous ruin, and if so that is ridiculous in our time when you can walk into any literary group and encoun-ter adherents of Oscar's sexual preference who not only do not conceal it but even proclaim it.

LET'S TRY this. . . . Poetry attracts the self-pitying type both as reader and practitioner. Why? In all the going terms of contemporary life poetry is a failure. Only the few (the "special") people want it. In these terms poetry is, therefore, "other than" all the accepted, successful, necessary things. To be devoted to it sets one apart. To spend a lifetime trying to write it removes one—all the cant within poetry circles to the contrary—from competition. "Competition" between contemporary poets is a fiction. Just because it is believed in and acted upon does not make it real. Confusion over these matters is confusion of fame. No man's "success" as a poet diminishes my own or mitigates my failure. Poetry has to be done in retreat from the world to deal with the world. Therefore the privacy—specialness—ego—self-absorption—(it may be) self-pity. All poetry is worked within one's self but it is not good unless it projects meaningfully into others' lives. This is not the only, the ultimate test, since all sentimental verse projects movingly into many lives. But good poetry projects permanently into others' lives. Now a few in one century—maybe thousands in another century—maybe fading back again after that—but always renewing and therefore being renewed. The necessary arrogance of the artist is the other side, the healthy side, of self-pity. Self-pity is the shortsighted view of it all, the perversion of it, the sickness of it.

•

TRY, IN NEW poems, for subjects—events—situations—new to your verse. Such may awaken vocabulary you have not hitherto used, and freshen your style; may even, in a desert stretch, renew you and your verse. (But this must be tried seriously, not meretriciously; it is not easy.)

126

POETRY IS the uninhibited child standing up at the edge of the crowd and saying what they could not or would not say, or did not know enough to say.

•

LANGUAGE IS everything. Reading Delmore Schwartz's poems in considerable bulk, I kept asking What is wrong with these?—and decided the fault is in their commonplace language: no freshness—no tension, no excitement.

•

IN EVERY GENERATION there are great minds—minds that open new areas in science, in philosophy, in government: that discover new methods, new answers: that invent, that make new formulas—minds, a relative handful, that take the whole human race further along. In each generation, also, there is usually a great poet or two. And what is the characteristic of a poet's mind? A curious ability when using one word to think of another which sounds well with it. The ability is not only curious, it is almost unconscious. (I know poetry does many other things—but this is the basic, the thing the man is born with.) Can we rank this childlike mind with such other greats as Aristotle, Einstein, and whomever you want to name in between? It would not seem so. But there is a joker in the pack. Theories of government, philosophies, religions, rise and fall and fade away; science continually makes obsolete its old answers with its new; etc.; but poetry persists, endures. The Greek religion of ancient times is now a myth—but Homer is not outdated.

TO MAKE the *fact* into the poem.

●

FOR THE ARTIST: Work honestly every day—every day that you can—and perhaps when you are old (and dead) there will be a structure (which you can never foresee) that is the shape of your life. And it will have substance, meaning, consequence. This is not given to most human beings—it is possible to the relative few. It can be achieved only through this semi-blind process of honestly working, the best you can; and there is no guarantee even at that. But also there is no other choice of any significance.

●

Book of Poems 1959

Here is the poet, out in paperback,
Just like Spillane and Kerouac.
Let opinions on its merits vary—
His worry: it looks so temporary.

●

The Novel

Writing's attained to a new condition
Which really amounts to superstition:
Its sins are all the sins of emission.

AS TO Roy Campbell. Byronism was outrageous in its own time, in ours it is embarrassingly preposterous. (But he did write that quatrain asking "Where's the bloody horse?")

•

ABOUT TALKING about one's published poems—I so often forget the circumstances which, later, interest some people. Still the rule is: intensity while approaching the poem, a greater intensity while writing it; then—usually for a brief span—a cool concentration while revising. After that all the rest can as well drop away, as so much scaffolding from a completed building. (Or: cf. writing a poem to modeling in clay.)

•

Mulling Over The Engle-Spangle

Comes with his poems up from the meadows,
Up from those lustily,
            gustily American meadows,
In which he was so lucky to be spang-
            middle born,
Comes with his poems, star-bannered, rich
            with corn.

•

TEACHING: to be *there* when the "wild surmise" happens.

I WONDER how many millions of dollars Shakespeare has made for other people?

•

IN WRITING—cut the fat, cut the fat—that at times can be so rosily luscious.

•

CRITICISM and poetry. The Anatomist and the Lover. Let's admit a man may be both. But let us remember there is no connection between the dissection table and the nuptial bed.

•

Poetry

Novelists who have truck with it
Always end up in the muck with it.
So it follows
That us fellows
Who write the stuff are stuck with it.

•

SO MANY WRITERS *start* as poets that it might be argued those who stick with poetry are cases of arrested development.

(ESSIE BATES says that Elinor Wylie had "a terrible figure.")

●

THE TROUBLE with Conrad Aiken's poetry is, he's all lips and no teeth.

●

ROBINSON'S "Flammonde"—is it a (probably unconscious) auto-biographical projection? ". . . his fee/ To live, he borrowed graciously." A sort of day-dream justification of EAR?

●

The Literary World

The sense of this world is shit:
Long—not various—its exhibit:
To review and be reviewed.

●

THIS IS interesting and curious: most publishers will "do" a book *about* poetry at the drop of a hat—in contrast to their reluctant (to put it gently) attitude toward a book of poetry. Why? I think the answer involves more than poetry—that this is symptomatic of the contemporary mind, which prefers to read *about* things rather than to experience things. Prose—in other words—not poetry.

I NOTICE in a *London Times* Literary Supplement review of a book on Cummings the observation that if you move from the *evocative* to the *persuasive* you move "dangerously close to the old Greek definition of rhetoric."

•

THE "GERRY TYPE." See my review of the biography of John Middleton Murry. I should have said something about a boyish helplessness masking a most rigid pig-headedness. He drops lighted matches all over the house, and when the whole place is really going up and the other inhabitants desperate to get out—he is coolly strolling off, some blocks away, asking what the sirens are all about. Usually on his way to another house, and another woman; by prearrangement.

•

THE PROFESSORS of poetry aren't really interested in poetry— they are interested in bibliography.

•

VACHEL LINDSAY (again):—his "big" poems are really libretti. If Horace Gregory is right about the disappearance of Amy Lowell's poems with *her* disappearance from the public platform, how much truer in Lindsay's case.

•

THAT HALLMARK CARD *contract*: ". . . Winfield Townley Scott (hereinafter known as 'Poet')" . . .

IN HER NOVEL, *Bid Me to Live*, H.D. says, ". . . another substance but the same, as ice, as steam, as water are also the same yet three states." This is an excellent image for what I have tried to say about the line in narrative poetry. In the long poem you must skirt prose—keep the story going—have people talk believably—rise to passionate poetry in speech and description—and yet, and yet it must be the same line, the same poem.

•

WHAT CONRAD KNICKERBOCKER said about my poem "Watch Hill": "My God! That *s l o w* hard-on!"

•

THE AGE of the mask. The public figure whose speeches—that is, his public expression and therefore public image—are written for him. . . . This could be pursued deeply. A kind of immorality, even? Certainly a sort of deception. And a symbol of the out-of-focus era in which we live. —For contrasting example: what would Lincoln represent—what would Lincoln *be*—if we knew that the Gettysburg Address and the Second Inaugural were written by John Hay?

•

PAUL HORGAN to me that Robert Lowell, reading at Wesleyan University last spring, said, "Gentlemen, when I say 'stuffed duck' in a poem I *mean* 'stuffed duck.' I don't mean anything else." Bravo!

WE HAVE to live *our* generation—and know it is in all important essentials *any* generation; that we need not look before and after and pine for what is not. All life exists at any time; all love, all sorrow and failure, all tragedy and joy—these recur; if we live we do not miss anything.

●

IN POETRY there are never "new subjects." Think of the era when it was machines or prizefights—or political programs—as *subjects*. You can go *through* "new" things—automobiles or atomic bombs—but only to the everlasting human values. . . . Keats felt no need to write of hansom cabs. . . . (What about E. Dickinson and the train?)

●

THE TROUBLE with the usual social intercourse is that the person one most truly is is not brought into play. Instead all the superficial amenities. That is not you I'm talking to, this is not me you are talking to. For such would not be a party. It is very tiring because one is playing a part—not insincerely necessarily, though I think that is the increasing danger as time goes on—but (as when a writer is not writing) one gets so out of touch with one's self.

●

YVOR WINTERS. His criticism is innocently dishonest, the work of a small writer who attempts to tear down all big writers and in the same process elevate a few other tiny writers. The real purpose is pathetic: to exalt by inference his own value as a poet. Of course it won't succeed but it can do a great deal of harm to young and impressionable minds.

●

THE CONCEIT of the young is more forgivable, being not so sure of itself, than the vanity of the old.

●

THE PRICE of literary talent is chronic indigestion.

●

IF A MAN WRITES a great book between twenty and thirty, best for him that the fact go unrecognized—whether it's a small great book like *The Red Badge of Courage* or a big great book like *Moby-Dick*. Better confusion and silence than all the prizes at that early age.

●

ELIZABETH BESTON the other day said she feels a stress in my poetry—Southwest landscape pulling this way, New England landscape pulling that way; and was she correct, and what was my inclination? I said: Correct, and that though I had done no poetry for months, all my thinking in terms of landscape was now New England. (Remember what I so arrogantly said about living in the Southwest.)

●

(THE RECORD: since I last typed out the paragraphs I from time to time scribble for this book, I have been chiefly busy with a book of essays, *Exiles and Fabrications,* published last August, and with work on my collected verse, *Poems: 1937–1962,* scheduled for next spring. . . . But I have new poems—perhaps at least half a book—which I am holding back.)

●

PERHAPS "IDEAS" get nowhere for poems unless you have a controlling Idea. And what have I ever clung to except the conviction that life is all and that death gives life its significance? Is that enough?

●

AS THE YEARS go by, one grows so mad to try to write well that the desire comes to have a moral basis.

●

WHY SHOULDN'T these younger men use Bill Williams' latter-day three-steps-down "stanza"? Not merely because they can't

do it so well, but because it isn't really a form—it is an emana-
tion of WCW's style. I don't see how it can be employed by
others and not remain imitation.

•

The Aging Husband

The ardent girl he used to lay
Is now content to skip or skim it.
In committee work she goes the limit.
She is fulfilled by PTA.

•

WHAT IS the explanation of nostalgia in American art? (I am
not about to answer this.) I have just been listening to Aaron
Copland's *Appalachian Spring* and the sweet, beautiful theme
is as haunting and lonesome and longing as—well, *Tom Sawyer*
and *Huckleberry Finn* and *Moby-Dick* and *The Scarlet Letter*
and *Our Town,* etc., etc. Why is it that we, the youngest great
nation in the world, have made our most beautiful work out
of the poignancies of the past? To what extent are we sentimental? (By the way, speaking of music: cf. a greater piece, Ives's
Second Symphony and the heartbreaking theme in that.)

My impulse is to read only American books now—to reread
Emerson, Thoreau, Whitman—all the rest—to be soaked in our
own past—to become as powerfully provincial as Yeats.

•

FROST'S POPULARITY—is it because his poems are basically story
poems?

ROBERT HILLYER, attacking the Pound-Eliot era in poetry, has said we must get poetry out of the library and into the fresh air again. At first glance this strikes me as a telling blow. But consider the point of view: Hillyer himself, as poet, is merely down in another stack of the library.

●

VIRGIL THOMSON'S crack, that the trouble with being a poet is what to do with the other twenty-three and a half hours a day.

●

STRAVINSKY HAS a good phrase when, speaking of his musical intentions, he espouses the "rejection of the spectacular." Cf. my belief (already noted) that in art we don't want the extraordinary—we want the ordinary made dramatic and meaningful. Add: Hindemith's remark that the only question is, is the music "genuine"?

●

Widows

The widows of minor writers are more touching
Than the widows of major writers. Both are
    annoying.
But the widows of minor writers grow so
    thinned
Cupping their hands around flickering flame
    in a high wind.

WE SHOULD have too much love—or at least, respect—for older poems to snatch lines from them, either to quote or misquote in poems of our own. We should, in writing, have such zeal for the inexhaustible intricacies of our own language to refrain from appropriating lines and phrases out of other languages.

•

IN WRITING prose: to write as well as I can I have to ride the escalator which is the emotional underpinning; otherwise it's plodding up a stairway—i.e., as I might try to write objective higher criticism, which I don't do well; indeed don't do at all. It is in this of course that my prose relates closely to my verse. (This is merely a personal statement, not an adage for anybody else.)

•

IF YOU CARE passionately for some phase of the arts, know as soon as you can that you belong to a minority—so you will not waste time and energy in worry about that .

•

VARIOUS CREATIVE processes really do have something in common. At my age (fifty-one) I may slide along for a couple of weeks without sex, but then when I have some for a while I want some more—the next day, and the next. Same with writing poems. . . . Also you can no more *force* poems than you can force sexual desire.

A YOUNG CONTRIBUTOR to *Poetry* (Chicago) declares that he is at work on a novel "which," he says, "*because of its subject can never be printed*."

•

I HEARD a man on radio describe writing as "the riskiest way to make a living since gladiators."

•

I'VE BEEN READING and re-reading some of Dick Eberhart's poems. I confess to this bafflement: for once at least I cannot tell where naïveté leaves off and where genius begins.

•

The New Yorker slates me in a paragraph on *Exiles and Fabrications* for the fault of overenthusiasm. In the same issue the drama review begins: "This play cannot possibly be as good as I think it is." Well—there's the choice of how you want to live.

•

WHAT SO MANY of these current formal poets indulge in is mere poetic calisthenics.

•

ONE FAMOUS AMERICAN family seems fated to contribute, every generation, a prominent poet—and each time over-rated.

ONE HAS to learn to trust one's self. That sounds simple-minded perhaps. But I think it isn't. In the long run it is all one can do.

•

OF COURSE, it is hard for a poet to tell when he is being lazy and when he is wisely not—as he should not be—forcing the issue.

•

MY TERRIBLE and depressing dismay—on the eve of my fifty-second birthday—to rediscover that was Shakespeare's age when he died.

•

WIVES OF WRITERS are wanted in so many ways by writers—and in some ways are not needed at all. There's the trouble.

•

BEWARE OF ALL poems serving public occasions.

•

YEATS IN MIDDLE-AGE learned from young Pound and hardened his style. But note: it was his own style he hardened—he did not write like Pound. . . . Incidentally, is this not a rare thing: the greater poet (so I assume) learning from the lesser?

•

I'VE BEEN READING (1962) the current issue of a little magazine called *Coastlines*. Free verse. Haiku. Poems called Cantos (à la Pound) and written à la Williams. An article which approvingly quotes Amy Lowell on poetry as excitement of the consciousness: that about says everything, the author concludes. —Well, for heaven's sake! These young "experimentalists" are forty years back. This is where I came in.

•

JOSEPH WOOD KRUTCH: he reassures one, in his search for values, about not being too bloody urban as a poet.

•

I HAVE just read Calvin Hoffman's *The Murder of the Man Who Was Shakespeare*. It has given me pause. Hoffman's theorized story is fantastic; but is it implausible? Is it more plausible than the sudden emergence after Marlowe's alleged death of the hitherto unknown William Shakespeare? . . . Certainly one can say this: his is the only anti-Shakespeare theory worth considering. It involves a known great poet. . . . I'm torn between fascination and shame that after all these years I should even consider giving over my scorn of the anti-Stratfordians. Well, I retain most of the scorn—scorn for all the DeVereites, Baconians, all of the lot. But Marlowe? But Marlowe?

•

SAMUEL JOHNSON is often amusing and sometimes, I suppose, admirable. But how can one ever like him? He embodies all the worst English traits—all the bombastic arrogance, all the insular rudeness. (I've been reading not Boswell but Krutch.) And when all's said and done, the old prejudice is correct: Johnson *does* survive by biography and not by his own writing.

•

IN WRITING—as indeed in life—one should not strive to be charming.

•

FOR SOME REASON it is unwise for poetry to deal in futurities. "I will go down to the sea again" etc. It seldom carries conviction as poetry. Is it because poetry should seem basically so factual?

•

THE DRAMATIST *manqué* is not to be found only among poets. You find him, for instance, among biographers; and superbly, for instance, in Lytton Strachey. I have been re-reading Strachey's

143

books and I find them dazzling. Mencken was fond of pointing out that not Strachey but Gamaliel Bradford invented the "psychograph"; but, alas for America, Bradford was no such stylist as the Englishman—he can't touch him. . . . But—as to the dramatist take, just in *Elizabeth and Essex*, the gorgeous pages describing King Philip of Spain at work in his room: the old man is merely doing just that—incessantly working at his papers, at his desk; but, ah, it is "as good as a play." Or—of course—toward the end of her life, Elizabeth's magnificent speech of love to the delegates from Commons: Strachey interrupts it—adds—just touches it a few times, and in just such vibrant ways as to heighten the drama. He *stages* it.

●

READING Carl Sandburg's new poems (and glancing back at the great bulk of the old ones) : No. You cannot be that loose, that dreamy, that imprecise, and write poetry.

●

HOW OFTEN in rewriting one alters from "book" English to spoken.

●

IN ROBINSON, when the laconic habit is carried too far—when, simply, we are not told enough—significance is lost. A sort of teasing coyness occurs.

AN ELDERLY COUPLE came up to me the other night after my reading in Kansas City and the lady said, "May we give you some advice? —Don't refer so often to your age. You're not old. And think how it makes us feel." . . . Watch this not only in talking but in new poems?

●

KEEP READING the dictionary. Sometimes an entire poem emerges from discovery of what one word really means.

●

QUALITY. In art quality is everything. Yet in general it is likely to emerge from a great deal of quantity. Is that clear? I mean the greatest poets are almost invariably prolific.

●

THE CHINESE would make this the poem:

> Magic casements
> Open on foam
> Of long-forgotten seas
> In forlorn faerylands.

But we want in English-American tradition more than that. We are not content with the isolated image. We want other, relevant images that make an architectural whole; and a musical whole. We prefer a bulge of language.

CONTRAST "business ethics" and the ethics of art. Nobody writes a poem hoping it will wear out in four or five years.

•

IF THE IMPULSE is genuine will its expression in art therefore be genuine? Not necessarily—not at all necessarily.

•

I AM INTERESTED in how the mind when it livens up with a new writing project simultaneously opens up to other writing possibilities. This has happened to me many times, but let me be specific. For more than three months I have been in that miserable, deadly state of being unable to write. As always, poems are inconceivable—and I court sleep, alcohol—I am wretched, irritable, utterly defeated: one doubts everything one has ever written and looks away with despair from the future. Nerves grow rampant. Now today I have begun research and note-taking for an essay on the town of Chimayo; and not only have I had an increasingly exciting day as I began to touch some of the form and some of the phrasing of the piece (for much of which I am still ignorant) but—extraneously—I have noted ideas, phrases, for possible poems. One's mind, beginning to work on *this*, seems to reach out toward *that*—and *that*. I begin to live again.

I admit: this is still not poems, and there can be—probably there is—hopeful illusion going on; but the feeling is one of stilled wheels turning again, and that feeling is invigorating, wonderful.

I wish I would remember—look forward—wait for this in the dead stretches; but I never can.

Everything one hears, feels, smells, touches, thinks seems suggestive—alive with possibilities. I am resurrected.

Response is all.

●

NOT TO MAKE something "beautiful" but something true—which in time will be beautiful.

●

I SAID to Vera Zorina the other night at a party, "I admire you so much that I am shy of you. And that's silly, isn't it?" She said, "Yes, it is silly, and several times in my life I have felt the same way." (Evidentally superb beauty is not necessarily an armor.)

●

I AM FOREVER quoting French writers—they say such honest things.

●

DURING THE INTERMISSION at Berg's opera *Lulu*, Lawrence Powell said, "This is the way Strauss used to sound to people who know nothing about music."

SPEAKING OF a homosexual singer who seemed to him inadequate as the male lead in an opera, Rudolf Heinrich said, "You cannot imitate a man."

●

AT FIFTY-THREE I look back across many years and in confusion. So much to remember, but now it all seems chaotic. I can make no shape, continuity, out of it; no meaning. Are these utter disconnections related to my inability to write these past five months? I think probably: I think that, when one is writing, a center—at least the illusion of a center—is created. Otherwise "things fall apart."

●

FROST NEVER kept a notebook. He believed that poems should emerge without scaffolding. As an inveterate note-maker (but not *these* notes—another kind), I sense the danger of letting it go at that: over many years one might get fulfillment just out of notes. Nonetheless through these many years (that is, since my youthful poems) I have rarely written a poem that did not have its start in a note—or, mostly, in two or more notes mating.

When I cannot write poems I feel like a singer who has lost his voice—and with it his excuse for being.

I lead a bourgeois life—wife, children, a rather big house—all that—plenty of money. Poetry out of this enviornment? One's mind and heart can supply sufficient suffering anywhere.

MISS MERRILL—to me—in High School Freshman Latin: "Well —you don't know anything! Sit down!"

●

DIRECT CONNECTION between what you do—how much money you make—and what you *have*. Ninety-eight percent of people thus. But I have been removed from this for nearly twenty years. Consider effects. Reality?

●

PAIN enforces a reality.

●

IN YOUNG YEARS flesh overcomes spirit. Later—is it spirit overcoming flesh? (I think not, though at times it may be true. But the victory is more by default: the failing of flesh.)

●

ALVAREZ—here from London the other day—says Robert Lowell represents "a new sensibility—a new step forward such as we had with Eliot."

ENGLISH CRITICS of American poetry strike me as prone to miss the most—or rather to under-rate the most—characteristically American poetry. They get the rather French-like Stevens. The accent is odd, but in Frost they have the greatest of the Georgians. But they can't really hear and evaluate a W. C. Williams.

•

ELIOT, POUND, and Longfellow are technically international. Ponder this as to eventual status of E. and P.

•

I WANT to start with a room—a house—a street corner—a town —a city—and see if I can be taken from there.

•

TO WHAT SELF does one discount one's self?

•

HE LIGHTS a pipe and in his hairy tweed suit sighs back against the upholstered wing chair by the fireplace where the mulled ale is kept warm on the hearth and he quotes to a few academic companions, "Of the making of books there is no end." And they nod and twinkle in silent assent. This is (or was: am I old-style?) the Literary Atmosphere.

—God save me. God save us all.

NOTES—notes—notes—but where's the symphony?

•

AT FIFTY-FOUR does one have to go on trying to write? So many writers died so much younger—ten, twenty, thirty years younger —shucked off the burden.

•

SEX: two dogs on a front lawn.

•

BILL WILLIAMS: "I could not write without form."

•

HEMINGWAY SAYS—to try each day to put down one thing you know is true.

•

THOSE whose favorite poetry is something soothing.

•

GRAHAM GREENE: "It needs a very strong man to survive an introspective and solitary vocation."

IT FREQUENTLY REQUIRES a major effort to write even minor verse.

•

HE ENTERED upon the writing of poetry as though it were the undertaking business.

•

THE POETRY-WRITING youngsters these days settle for so little. (I mean they "get" the quick notation of a W. C. Williams—or think they do—and that's all they get.)

•

I AM SORRY for people who are always busy. Apparently they have nothing better to do.

•

BILL WILLIAMS to the contrary, that five-beat line—iambic—can shift its stresses all over the place—and still be a real line and a continuing, flowing line—and take its tone from ordinary American speech.

•

THE INADVERTENT obscenities of the innocent (as in Dickinson, "Wild nights" etc., and in Hopkins' "Over again I feel thy finger and find thee.") See also Melville's *Pierre* where the half-sister cries to P. "My bed! Lay me! Lay me!" (Though here of course another matter than innocence—in M.'s time that verb evidently was not used as in ours).

•

THE TROUBLE with R. is that she hasn't written poems—she has developed projects. And look at Yevtushenko: he produces not poems but public speeches.

•

ALMOST ALL poems are failures. But one must never think—one never thinks—of this when one is writing a poem. And no doubt this goes—as usual—for painting and all the arts.

•

DELIBERATION in poetry—like garters—must never show. (Cf. Poe, etc.)

•

I OFTEN HASTEN to inform people that "I am not an intellectual," when I'd better just let them hang around and they'll find out for themselves. (To say such a thing may be in hopes the hearer will protest.)

OF SO-AND-SO: He is a very extinguished poet.

•

BY REVISION, I think I saved that poem but it may be a basket case.

•

"SO I TRANSFORM myself into a dial, and my shadow will tell me
where the sun is."   Emerson

•

I TOLD a poet his ego is blasphemous. He didn't seem to understand me.

•

OR PUT IT this way. An "idea" for a poem is a magnet—not in
itself sufficient to become a poem. But once you have it, you move
it about in search of iron filings.

"Love is not love / Which alters when it alteration finds."
There is an example of poetry which has no images—which
makes an abstract statement. But it makes it with that concentration of language basic to poetry and so it is poetry.

•

X'S INSUBSTANTIAL POEMS—trying to understand them: I'd as
soon try to put fog in a box.

DOUGLAS (ALMOST SEVEN) has taken to writing little three or four sentence "stories" which he refers to as "poems." Last night he looked up from his labors at the kitchen table and said, "I find being a poet is fun, even though my poems are not very good."

●

THE CROWNS, after listening to my Yale recording, said—or rather, Hilliard said—that I am a sentimentalist and a Romantic. —A Romantic, yes; but I think not sentimental. To be sentimental is, as has been said, to display more emotion than the subject justifies. It is to say: Here is a one-hundred-dollar check of a poem, when there's only fifty dollars' worth to back it. This I don't think I do.

●

DAVID GREENHOOD, speaking of the current variations on meter and cadence, observes this puts an added burden on the reader's ear—an added difficulty. This comes home sharply to me, for my "experimentation" is chiefly—perhaps only—in shifting of accent; and I am irked by the conviction that people (most people) do not *hear* my poems. Only if I read them aloud. . . . I recall one reviewer regretting that there is "no music in Scott's poetry." Good God, there's music—sweet, harsh, dissonant—everywhere in it. This is perhaps the only thing I'm certain of about it.

●

THE FEELING of being off the main track—non-essential—of saying nothing to do with what is *basic* to our times; flirting with

buttercups while the whole world burns. Have I shut myself away
—not been aware enough—not lived enough?

•

SUBSTANCE IN POETRY seems to me increasingly important. What
we miss in minor poets is something *said*. I.e., in my time such
lyricists as (to pick on friends of mine) Bynner and Hillyer:
fundamentally we are disappointed because the things they say
are so slight. . . . And myself?

•

BECAUSE DICKINSON lived in Amherst we have the town as *it*
lived and moved and had its being during the nineteenth century.
We know it as if we had been to a play or read a long novel. Especially (Jay Leyda's two volumes) when we read around her
—the scaffolding. . . . A lot of Emily at one time—her letters—
can be enervating. Her whimsy—her way of not saying the
simple fact. Her obsession with death—somewhat excusable as
friends and relatives died—is sickened by her reaching out for
reports of "last hours"—deathbed details.

•

I SEE NOW that in writing poetry I think in sounds. In a way this
seems to operate below the level of consciousness. At least, one
sees the patterns after the poem is completed; and then may consciously thicken the mixture.

TIM REYNOLDS and Charles Stein discussing this "breath" business controlling the line in verse. (This, I gather, is the doctrine according to Charles Olson.) I asked how the theory differed from Amy Lowell's and the other *vers librists* of fifty years ago. Well—somehow Stein thought it must. Arrangement of lines and words on the page are also, he said, a guide to the proper reading of the poem. But this, he said, has nothing to do with Cummings. . . . I suppose most young poets have the conviction they have discovered principles hitherto unknown. They are so bright and quick and certain—and I feel slow-minded and uncertain. . . . Oh, it appears too that there are those who maintain that the typewriter influences—or should influence—the length of the poetic line. God knows in what way or why.

●

I HAVE NEVER written a poem on a typewriter.

●

T. S. ELIOT in his last years saying, "I should like to write new poems, unlike those I have written." I wonder what he had in mind?

●

A MAN MAY write a poem with his fly blatantly open—but the blatancy must not be in the poem.

WITH A JUST-FINISHED poem: I set it on the windowsill and every now and then check to see if it is jelling and how its color looks in the sun.

●

Note Left

Sex
Art
Death.

Should I weave
An acrostic
Daring us both to read my three
themes spelled out?

INDEX

Wilson, Edmund, 96
Winters, Yvor, 12, 134–135
Wright, Frank Lloyd, 3
Writer in America, The, 69

Yeats, William Butler, 6, 8–9, 28, 36,
43, 52, 74, 77, 84, 90, 100–101, 107,
141–142